Haile Selassie I

Ethiopia's Lion
of Judah

Books by Peter Schwab

Haile Selassie I: Ethiopia's Lion of Judah (1979)
Human Rights: Cultural and Ideological Perspectives (1979)
  (co-author and co-editor)
Is America Necessary? (1976) (co-author)
John F. Kennedy (1974) (co-author)
Decision Making in Ethiopia: A Study of the Political Process
  (1972)
Ethiopia and Haile Selassie (1972) (editor)
Biafra (1971) (editor)
Greece Under the Junta (1970) (co-editor)

Haile Selassie I

Ethiopia's Lion of Judah

Peter Schwab

Nelson-Hall nh Chicago

Library of Congress Cataloging in Publication Data

Schwab, Peter, 1940-
  Haile Selassie I: Ethiopia's Lion of Judah.

  Bibliography: p.
  Includes index.
  1. Haile Selassie I, Emperor of Ethiopia, 1891-1975.
2. Ethiopia—History—1889-1974. 3. Ethiopia—History—
Revolution, 1974. 4. Ethiopia—Kings and rulers—
Biography.
DT387.7.S372   963′.05′0924   [B]   79-9897
ISBN 0-88229-342-7

Manufactured in the United States of America

10   9   8   7   6   5   4   3   2   1

Contents

Acknowledgments

This book has its origins in the year 1967 when I first visited Ethiopia on a Fulbright-Hays Grant. As a graduate student at the New School for Social Research I then embarked on a study of the feudal land system in Ethiopia and its implications for the political process. I became both fascinated and repelled by the political system then in existence under the authority of Emperor Haile Selassie. After another trip to Ethiopia in 1968, I proceeded to write my Ph.D. dissertation on the Ethiopian political system and thus began ten years of concentrating on and writing about Ethiopian politics. After receiving my degree in 1969 I returned to Ethiopia a number of times to update my research. Since then I have written extensively on Ethiopian politics and have recently concentrated on Ethiopia's political/military position in the Horn of Africa.

Throughout this period of time I have received constant encouragement from Adamantia Pollis, once my mentor at the New School and for the past ten years a close friend. She has always been a willing listener and an acute critic. There is no way I can ever convey to her my appreciation for her support.

Professors Christopher Clapham and John Markakis, both noted Ethiopianists, have often been supportive and helpful. Although I rarely see them now, I wish them to know that though their advice has sometimes been taken, sometimes discarded, the discussions and correspondence I have had with them about Ethiopia have been helpful, invigorating, and challenging. Another who has always been ready for lively debate and argument is Lee Shneidman and there has never been a time when he was not ready to talk late into the night about issues regarding Ethiopia. A close friend, he has unfailingly been a professional critic who always laced his words with the strongest support he could muster. If he is as good a teacher as he is critic and friend, his students are very fortunate indeed. Conalee Levine-Shneidman, a friend whom I respect and cherish, has been an aid of towering proportions. Her psychological skills and insights have been of extraordinary benefit to me, particularly in this book, and the finest compliment I can offer her is the knowledge that without her technical expertise, this book could not have been written.

Two other individuals, Eshetu Habtegiorgis and Abdulla Adem, were always there when I needed them. With the violence and havoc that presently exists in Ethiopia I don't know if they are dead or alive, in prison or out. I can only hope that they are free and that they can be made aware of the important role they played in my life in Ethiopia.

Among the institutions that afforded me the opportunity to broaden my knowledge of Ethiopia are Colgate University, Adelphi University, and The State University of New York, College at Purchase. All have funded me throughout the past ten years in terms of doing research in Ethiopia or in the United States. The United States Office of Education has also been most generous.

Annedorle Sreckovich has typed almost all my major manuscripts. She is an extremely adept professional who has been a true asset. The index for this book was prepared by Anita Altman.

This book, any book, is the accumulation of data and experience integrated with ideology, and in this process, I have profited from my relationship with many individuals. Although I do not wish to list them all I wish to thank them all. They know who they are.

1. Scholarly Research on Ethiopia under Haile Selassie's Rule

In 1976 Alula Hidaru and Dessalegn Rahmato observed that a "person who starts out to make even the most casual investigation of Ethiopia is immediately confronted with a host of obstacles. The most serious of these is the paucity of reliable information on virtually any aspect of the country."[1] They go on to say that both

> Ethiopian and foreign writers are responsible in this regard. The foreign writer, either because of some kind of loyalty to the Ethiopian government or out of what can only be considered a false sense of affection for the country, invariably goes out of his or her way to present a favourable, and oftentimes, a rosy picture of Ethiopia. On the other hand, there is great pressure on the Ethiopian writer not only to avoid criticism but also not to be miserly in his praise of the society and the power-holders. The threat of rejection of his work by the government-controlled printing establishments and serious persecution usually assures that the Ethiopian writer will not over-step the bounds marked out for him.[2]

Prior to the 1970s Ethiopia was indeed the neglected stepchild of academics studying Africa, and the above statement would have been valid. But in the 1970s a substantial body of published material became available to social scientists, and without question much of it is excellent. In political science, sociology, economics, and anthropology, contemporary Ethiopia has been analyzed, and the dynamics of the social/political system have been written about. Today, a student of Ethiopia can go to the library and successfully seek out data on the Ethiopian political/economic system[3], on land tenure arrangements[4], on individual ethnic groups[5], on civil and revolutionary disturbances[6], and on the social relationships among

1

and between peoples.[7] And unlike the era prior to the 1970s these works are substantial, analytical, and critical, and encompass conservative, liberal, radical, and Marxist ideology.

It was no accident that Ethiopia went generally unreported on in the first two decades after World War II. For this was the era of major nationalist movements in Africa, when leaders such as Kwame Nkrumah of Ghana, Sekou Toure of Guinea/Conakry, and Jomo Kenyatta of Kenya were organizing mass political movements in an attempt to expel their colonial overlords. American and European academics, fascinated with such agitation, and having access to foundation or government grants, flocked to these centers of nationalism accumulating their data and publishing their findings. Governments in Europe and in the United States were extremely concerned and worried that these nationalist leaders would alter the political and economic status quo. Because there was a paucity of data available on these new movements, the Western governments funded scholars, and even supported many of them in publishing their findings, so that Western political elites could make policy based on the findings of academics. As Marvin Surkin and Alan Wolfe have said:

> Research was being used not to serve the interests of the poor and oppressed around the world but rather to serve the interests of the U.S. government and the corporate establishment, for whom political science research was a most valuable tool.[8]

This, of course, is not to say that all works of this period were written expressly to advance the cause of the West. But a combination of academic interest in nationalist movements and governmental interest in the effect of these movements brought about an unusual concentration of research in areas where violence or potential violence might occur.

This left Ethiopia out in the academic cold. For the country was ruled by a man who had been in power since 1916 and it appeared that Emperor Haile Selassie had the political and social system under tight rein. The United States felt politically secure in Ethiopia, believed it was aware of all the possible variables that might alter the political situation, and saw little reason to subsidize scholars. Haile Selassie, dominating the feudal and totalitarian structure, had no interest whatsoever in allowing critical scholars to come to

Ethiopia and freely uncover what Ethiopia was really all about. Western social scientists had little interest in a country they often considered politically irrelevant. So unless the work was benign, related purely to history prior to Haile Selassie, or advanced his image, the emperor refused to allow scholars into the country. Western Europe and the United States offered few grants to travel there, and scholars themselves were uninterested in pursuing research in Ethiopia. Published books in the 1950s dealt essentially with Ghana, Kenya, Nigeria, or with the history of the continent or territories within it.

The scholarly situation began to change drastically in the 1960s, and there were three reasons for it. First, secessionist war between Ethiopia and its province of Eritrea was initiated in 1962 and the political/military implications were far-reaching since the United States had a military base in Asmara, the capital city of Eritrea. Second, Haile Selassie, born in 1892, was growing old, and the question of succession became important after an abortive 1960 coup and related directly to the future stability of Ethiopia. A combination of these two factors brought foundations and the United States government around to awarding grants and scholarships for Ethiopian research. The third cause of increased interest had to do with the fact that it became pointedly clear that very little real knowledge existed regarding the Ethiopian social system. As a result both Western and Ethiopian scholars intensified their scholarly work. With increased pressure from academics and from ruling circles in the West, Haile Selassie permitted a small number of scholars to pursue field work. After this period a spate of books appeared, and Ethiopian studies, a phenomenon of the past ten years, were born. Formal programs exist at the University of Chicago and at Northwestern University; books and articles about the country that are critical and scholarly continue to grow in number. With the present dispute between Ethiopia and Somalia over the Ogaden in which the United States and the Soviet Union are involved, even the general public is becoming aware of the presence of Ethiopia.[9]

But what can be said about Ethiopian studies cannot be said about Haile Selassie. There is almost no scholarly work of a

biographical nature available.[10] Despite the fact that he ruled
Ethiopia for fifty-eight years few writers have attempted to
analyze his leadership. Certainly, in analyses of Ethiopia he is
discussed and often at length. But the forces that made him
tick, the personal and emotional feelings that were part of him,
the man rather than the image, the particular flow of his existence have hardly been touched. And here Hidaru and
Rahmato are correct. With few exceptions historical works on
Haile Selassie are "usually accompanied by a generous dose
of high praise for the able leadership, wisdom and farsighted-
ness of the . . . emperor."[11]

Much of this was the emperor's own fault. An extremely
private and secretive man, he jealously guarded all aspects of
his personal life. There were almost no private confidants, and
when there were, they were prohibited from writing about
him. Whatever he has written has taken the form of public
speeches or extremely stilted and uninformative descriptions
of public events that he took part in. No letters or lengthy
personal remembrances of him by others exist. The protective
shell that he surrounded himself with to successfully create the
aura of noblesse oblige has prevented successful biography.
The lack of a free, open press also stymied the accumulation of
data. The media in Ethiopia during the reign of Haile Selassie
always reported his daily meetings with Ethiopian or diplomatic officials, but never were permitted to print anything of
substance. "The government censors all materials printed in
Ethiopia; since there are fewer than a dozen printing presses in
the country, some of them government-owned, control is facili-
tated. Although there is no official index of forbidden books,
books critical of the country are rarely sold publicly."[12] Haile
Selassie brought upon himself the inadequate and often purely
sycophantic literature dealing with his life.

There is one portion of his life that has been documented
extremely well: that is the period from 1935 to 1941 when
Italy invaded and occupied Ethiopia and the emperor was
forced to flee the country. Prior to his exile in Great Britain, he
traveled to Geneva where on June 30, 1936, he warned the
League of Nations that the very existence of world peace was
at stake and that if the League did not collectively come to the
aid of Ethiopia, the League of Nations would founder and

World War II would be imminent.[13] The speech, which was stirring and prophetic, hurled him into the world's spotlight. It made him, at least for the moment, a world figure of tragic proportions. He elicited for himself world sympathy and respect, and from that time on he was remembered for that one single historical moment. In October 1963 when he visited Washington, President John F. Kennedy welcomed the emperor within the context of the League speech. "In welcoming His Majesty . . . we welcome a man whose place in history is already assured. His memorable and distinctive appearance before the League of Nations in the mid-thirties . . . so stirred the conscience of the world. . . ."[14]

Haile Selassie's activity during this period is well reported, at least relative to other events. It was a momentous time for him, and because he was outside Ethiopia access to him was easier and therefore material is available.

Only a few published biographies on Haile Selassie exist, and no one of them extends throughout the full period of his life. The paucity of literature and the lack of biographical completion demands that a full biography be written, and that is the reason for this book. It is necessary and timely. Haile Selassie was the ruler of a social system that was oppressive to the peasants and tenant farmers who made up most of the population of the country and extremely beneficial to those few landlords that made up the ruling class. And although the emperor tried periodically to temper the abuses of the system, he never tried to reform it absolutely as that would have caused the destruction of the system. On the other hand, in international affairs, Haile Selassie's role was quite different and he was perceived as being an important African and international statesman. The subtleties and contradictions of Haile Selassie will be analyzed in this book. He was many things to many people and his various stances will be investigated.

But this is not just a biography of the leader of a country; it will touch on events both in and out of Ethiopia. Haile Selassie ruled one of the largest countries in Africa and one of the most ancient; he was in power longer than any other African statesman; he was involved in a series of international events covering more than five decades; he was extremely influential in initiating the Organization of African Unity; his good offices

were utilized numerous times to bring about the conclusion of
hostilities among a multiplicity of African states; and he was
without question the most famous contemporary monarch in
Africa.

Personally he was also distinctive. Secretive yet powerful,
he permitted few people to come close to him. Thus, reporting
on his life is challenging, particularly to a biographer. Many
leaders publicly air their individual warts and assets. This is
not the case with Haile Selassie. It is fascinating to read
accounts that major world leaders have written regarding their
meetings with the late emperor. Almost to a person, the accounts of his personality, his motivations, the essence of the
man are skimpy and vacuous. Although many have met him,
few, if any, seemed to know him. The most precise description
of this aspect of Haile Selassie's personality was rendered by
John Markakis.

> Despite the constant exposure of his person to his subjects, Haile
> Selassie has preserved an aura of awe-inspiring mystery which . . .
> thickens with the passage of years. Perpetually frozen into a posture
> of haughty regal isolation, the sombre figure of a ruler stands across a
> psychological divide which even his most trusted retainers cannot
> cross. Seen in the midst of his tense, scurrying courtiers, the diminu-
> tive Emperor gives the impression of remote aloofness and icy calm-
> ness that easily dominate any scene of which he is part. . . . Signifi-
> cantly, after more than fifty years of rule, Haile Selassie remains a
> mystery to his subjects. Little is ever known about his thoughts,
> which apparently are shared with no one. Rumours about the Em-
> peror's role, motivation, and interest in decisions abound, but facts
> about such matters are precious few.[15]

The material for this biography comes from primary and
secondary source material. In addition to the traditional
methods of research I have chosen to make extensive use of
the new academic currents that the field of psychohistory has
propounded. This is necessary if one is to make assumptions
and hypotheses about Haile Selassie's views and motivations.
As a research tool this mechanism is indispensable when dealing with a personage as private and mysterious as the emperor.
Although there is controversy as to the usefulness of psychohistory, its role in this analysis is necessary; what is more, as a
method of analysis it is as "objective" and impartial as any other
method. History is always seen from the perspective of the
beholder, and since all scholars harbor ideological predisposi-

tions, objectivity becomes a false idol. Therefore, a multiplicity of research methods has been utilized to produce this book, and each stands on equal level and validity with the others.

Haile Selassie I: Ethiopia's Lion of Judah will attempt to come to grips with the essence of the man and the monarch, and will analyze him within the perspective of major personal and political events that occurred throughout his life. The book will not concentrate on describing and analyzing all aspects of a particular issue, but will look at that issue in relation to Haile Selassie. For instance, a large body of literature already exists that scrupulously examines Italy's 1935 invasion of Ethiopia and I shall not attempt to review the entire spectrum of those events. What I will do is to scrutinize Haile Selassie's role therein, seeking to discover the factors that affected him on a personal, political, or diplomatic level. This book then can either stand on its own as biography or can serve to complement studies already written.

Haile Selassie was almost synonymous with contemporary Ethiopia, and his death in 1975 at the age of eighty-three, said to be due to the aftereffects of a prostate gland operation, marked the end of an era. Ruling Ethiopia almost as a medieval autocrat, he was for almost the entire span of his leadership the most powerful and dominant politician in the country. He was haughty and regal, totally in control of all decision-making, and at the pinnacle of an imperial palace structure so patrimonial that *all* others in the system, including his family, were regarded by Haile Selassie as retainers. Through a combination of charisma, patrimony, and feudalism, Haile Selassie maintained his imperial authority. He truly believed that his authority was bestowed upon him by God and that the positive qualities of all previous emperors had been transmitted to him by biological descent and by the act of consecration in which he was anointed head of the Ethiopian Orthodox Church.[16] Almost all members of the executive office or Imperial Palace had to consistently court his favor by daily appearing at the palace, fawning over him, and doing his bidding. One might lose power and authority by not showing proper fealty or by appearing too independent. Through a feudal system of land ownership, distribution, and land taxation, Haile Selassie prevented any mass opposition

from arising. A system of tenancy was created that made peasants almost the equivalent of serfs to the small percentage of
landowners, and the former, with some exceptions, were
almost totally at the mercy of the latter.

Until 1974 this charismatic/patrimonial/feudal system held
together. And Haile Selassie sat on top of it. He was such an
overwhelming figure inside and out of Ethiopia that it came as
a complete surprise to many when he was deposed, for it was
thought that surely he would be retained as a figurehead by
the new military junta. In fact, at a United States Department
of State colloquium on Ethiopia held in June 1974, three
months prior to the overthrow of Haile Selassie, all the participants maintained that Haile Selassie would not and could not
be removed from power because of the traditional legitimacy
with which he was perceived by his own population. How
wrong we all were!

This book will analyze the activities of Haile Selassie so as
to discern the variables that made him function as he did.
What was he like? Who was he? What direction had he in
mind for Ethiopia? What were the push and pull factors that
influenced him in terms of decision-making? What was his
true standing in international affairs? How did he perceive of
himself? What was his impact? How will history view him? It
is to these and other questions that this book will be directed.

2. The Ethiopian Context

Ethiopia, which is located in northeast Africa on a part of the continent known as The Horn, can be divided geographically into the highlands of the north and the lowlands of the south. About two-thirds of the land rises high above the lowlands to form part of the East African Rift Plateau. In Ethiopia its general elevation is 5,000 to 10,000 feet above sea level and it is dotted with high mountain ranges and cratered cones. Erosion has produced steep valleys and rapid waterways. The Great Rift Valley, the earth's most extensive fault, extends from Jordan to Mozambique. The portion that runs through Ethiopia is marked in the north by the Danakil Depression, a large triangular desert. In some places it is 300 feet below sea level and it is certainly one of the hottest places in the world. The northwest region of Ethiopia, around Addis Ababa, is also rugged plateau but its elevation is slightly lower. To the far north above the Danakil Depression is a ten- to fifty-mile-wide, hot, arid, coastal strip of land which leads to the Red Sea coast. Lake Tana, Ethiopia's largest lake, lies at the center of the highlands.

In contrast, the lowlands descending from the southwestern slopes of the Great Rift Valley are less abrupt and are broken by river exits. This leads to largely tropical lowland, sparsely populated. The southeast, in the arid Ogaden, is predominately semidesert.

All the country's rivers originate in the highlands and flow outward through gorges. Many are tributaries of the Nile system. The Blue Nile and its tributaries, together with the

Tekeze in the north and the Baro in the south, account for half
the outflow of water. The eastern part of the highlands is
drained by the Omo, while the great Awash River flowing
north from Addis Ababa disappears into the lakes of the
Danakil Depression. In the southeast the Wabi Shebeli
courses through the Somali Republic and into the Indian
Ocean.

Ethiopia, which has an estimated population of thirty million, is an extremely underdeveloped country economically
due in large part to the feudal land tenure system that has
existed for so long. Although much land lies completely unutilized, coffee is a major export crop accounting for the pro-
duction of more than 250,000 tons yearly. Addis Ababa, the
largest city in the country, is the capital, while Asmara, Dire
Dawa, and Harar make up the other urban centers. Addis
Ababa is, in fact, the hub of Ethiopia. In the last decades urban
immigration has been a strong force and the 1977 estimated
population is one and a half million. The city is a virtual mix of
ethnic groups with Amhara, Tigrai, Sidama, Galla, Muslims,
and Christians all represented.

The history of Ethiopia stretches over more than three
thousand years. During that time great empires such as Axum
and important emperors such as Menelik II (1889–1913) and
Haile Selassie I (1930–1974) played an important role in the
evolution of the country.

Once known as Abyssinia (the term is said to derive from the
Habashat, a South Arabian tribe that settled in East Africa),
Ethiopia is mentioned by both Homer and Herodotus and is
also referred to in the Old Testament. The Semitic settlers of
original Ethiopia arrived from Arabia in the first half of the first
millennium B.C., mixed with local Cushites, eventually organized themselves into the kingdom of Axum, and became a
dominant power in the Red Sea region. During the fourth
century A.D. these forbears of the people of Tigre were converted to Christianity, and Ezana, King of Axum, proclaimed
fealty to the Coptic Christian Church of Egypt that adhered to
the doctrine of Monophysitism, i.e., the belief that the human
and divine in Christ constitute only one nature. The new
religion, which became institutionalized in the Ethiopian Orthodox Church, evolved into an indigenous political and eco-

nomic power that all future emperors had to reckon with. Until the seventh century when it came into conflict with Islam, Axum flourished and expanded.

The Agau dynasty appeared during the period around 1137 and occupied the throne for a century. Its claim was contested by a group based in Shoa-Amhara province and tracing itself to King Solomon; in 1270 it established the Solomonic dynasty and proclaimed the Amhara region the political center of the state. Throughout the next few centuries the new dynasty spread its power and influence into the south and southeast sections of the plateau and consistently and often unsuccessfully battled incursions onto its territory first by Muslim forces, and then by the Oromo, or Galla as they are known in Ethiopia. After the sixteenth-century defeat of the Muslims who were intent on destroying the Christian stronghold, the Galla overran the territories of the south and southeast. Not until the nineteenth century were the Galla incorporated into the dominion of the Shoa. During the reign of Sahle Selassie (1813–47) Shoa took the south, west, and southeastern territories and the king proclaimed himself ruler of Shoa and of the Galla. Ethiopia enlarged its territory during the next fifty years under the dominance of emperors Theodore II, Yohannes IV, and Menelik II of Shoa who ruled from 1889 to 1913. It was during the reign of Menelik II that the empire was virtually doubled in size, leading to the creation of boundaries that have lasted, more or less, until today. In the process the Galla were thoroughly vanquished.

Ethiopia is the only state south of the Sahara that utilized classic techniques of imperialism and expansion through military conquest to determine its geographical boundaries. It is thus distinctive within Africa where all other states south of the Sahara have had their geographical limits established by European colonial powers.

The most dramatic and enduring myth had been utilized by the Solomonic dynasty to legitimate its rule; it is said that Sheba, Queen of Ethiopia, visited Solomon, King of Jerusalem, converted to Judaism and bore Solomon a son, Menelik I. The son later traveled from Ethiopia to Jerusalem to see his father whereupon he stole the ark of the covenant and returned home with it. Menelik I was considered related

to Christ through the holy man Solomon, since the latter two
were seen as the personification of God's will on earth, and the
Solomonic line of Ethiopian kings claimed the inheritance of
the theology upon Christ's rejection by the Jews and became a
Christian dynasty. Christianity and the mythical birth of
Menelik I were considered the roots of the Solomonic dynasty
in Ethiopia, both being utilized to legitimize its Divine Right
to the throne. Chapter One, Article Three of the 1931 Constitution, and Chapter One, Article Two of the 1955 Constitution translated this myth into legality, thus its importance to
the House of Solomon cannot be underrated.[1]

The populace of Ethiopia consists of two main groups,
Cushitic and Semitic. The latter and elements of the former
entered the area from Arabia. The Cushites include the Agaw,
Falasha (Ethiopian Jews), the Sidama of the southwest (which
includes Sidamo, Wolamo, and Kafa peoples), the Afar, Saho,
and Somalis. The Gallinya-speaking Galla are the largest
ethnic group of Cushitic peoples. The Semites consist of
Amhara and Tigrai, while a smaller group, known as the Shankella, are linked with the Nilotic peoples of southern Sudan.
Tigrinya, developed from the traditional and ancient Ge'es
language, is widely spoken in the north, as is Arabic. While
Amharic is the culturally predominant language, English and
Italian are spoken in government circles, the latter particularly
in Eritrea Province, until 1941 an Italian colony.

Historically, the country has been dominated by the
Shoan-Amhara who, together with other Amhara and the Tigrai, constitute about one-third of the population and inhabit
the northern provinces. Both the Amhara and Tigrai are
Ethiopian Orthodox (Coptic) Christians. The largest ethnic
group in Ethiopia are the Galla who make up some 40
percent of the population. Bound by a common language, they
live in the south. Those that reside close to the Muslim population in the east have adopted Islam as their own religion
while those living in the southwest have joined the Ethiopian
Orthodox Church. Although the Amhara and Tigrai are a
minority of the population they have politically dominated the
country. The Amharic culture has almost always been the
primary standard imposed whenever and wherever possible
on all other ethnic and religious groups. Amharic is the official

language of Ethiopia, while almost all the land in the country and almost all the political structures have been controlled by the Amhara and to some degree the Tigrai. The predominant ruling group, until 1974, was the Amhara who, centered in Shoa Province, were in fundamental control of the political system, the economic world, the military, and the Church.

The Ethiopian Orthodox Church, in existence since the fourth century, was, until the overthrow of Haile Selassie in 1974, the established church of the empire and its hierarchy is made up almost entirely of Amhara-Tigrai. Some 35 percent of the population are adherents to this theology. There are approximately the same percentage of Muslims in Ethiopia, a large number of whom live in Eritrea in the north. A much smaller number of peoples are made up of pagans, and a tiny Jewish group known as the Falasha who reside around the town of Gondar.[2]

So, despite the fact that Ethiopia is extraordinarily diverse in culture with a broad mix of ethnic groups and religions, the Amhara and the Christian Church have together controlled the political culture of the country more or less since the thirteenth century. They acted in unison to foster a policy of imperialism incorporating vast chunks of territory into the realm, and insofar as they were able, they prevented any other group from attaining power. Domestically they brought the Muslims, Galla, Sidama, Arussi, and Somali under their heel, and internationally they prevented other countries from establishing suzerainty over Ethiopia. The Turks, Portuguese, Egyptians, and under Menelik II the Italians, were all defeated in their attempts to establish themselves. Haile Selassie was both Amhara and Ethiopian Orthodox Christian and was strikingly representative in both his person and power of what the dual elements of that unified culture stood for.

Feudalism in Ethiopia[3] was the bedrock of the entire political and social system. Without the feudal structure the Shoa-Amhara would never have been able to control Ethiopia as long as they did. Status, class, and power were shaped by it and the political order was based upon it. The ruling class of contemporary Ethiopia was made up essentially of individuals who were responsible to or supportive of Haile Selassie. As the great warlords of the nineteenth century died off, Haile

Selassie appointed his comrades to positions in the central or local administration. Many were given large quantities of land as patronage and many were already large landholders. These landlords and government officials, together with the Ethiopian Orthodox Church, owned the bulk of the land in the country and controlled the everyday lives of the peasantry. This landed class imposed upon an oppressed class of tenant farmers a power hold in which the latter held no legal, political, or economic rights. Prior to the advent of Haile Selassie a feudal nobility also controlled the lives of peasants. Through tax and land tenure legislation initiated by Haile Selassie this feudal system was legitimized within the political structure.

The Ethiopian Orthodox Church is one of the most powerful and reactionary institutions in the country. Church ownership of land is rooted in the traditional right of emperors to grant lands to churches and monasteries and included tax privileges, a right which goes back to biblical times. Prior to 1974 the Church owned some 18 percent of the land in the country. Legally and traditionally exempt from the payment of land taxes, the Church, in 1942, was granted the statutory right to collect its own private taxes from its tenants, something it had traditionally always done in any case. Through tax collection, tax exemption, and rental of land, the Church evolved into a political, social, and economic power of unusually large dimensions.

Most of the land outside the provinces of Gojam, Tigre, and Beghemdir, where land is held communally, was owned by individual landlords, many who at one time or another held government positions and who maintained a rigid feudal relationship to tenant farmers. Through traditional and contemporary tax exemptions they remained almost totally free of land tax obligations, while at the same time they too were granted rights to privately and mercilessly tax their tenants. Traditional tax exemptions were often tied to individual rights to collect taxes. Under the *rist-gult* form of land tenure, granted since the Middle Ages by emperors to members of the royal family for services rendered, the landowner was entitled to collect and keep taxes under prescribed rates. *Maderia* land, granted to individuals in place of salary, was exempt from land tax, as was *Galla* land which was granted to landlords as pension. *Woqf* lands, granted to the Islamic Church, were also exempt from land taxes.

When land tenure did not call for exemption, landlords often illegally shifted the burden of payment of land taxes upon the tenant farmer. And since the tenant farmer held no functional legal rights, refusal to pay meant eviction. In addition landlords demanded at least 50 percent of the produce as rent, loaned money to tenant farmers at above 100 percent interest rates, demanded free services such as threshing, fencing, and herding of cattle, and collected a 10 percent tithe on produce that has been a traditional practice in Ethiopia since earliest times.

Under Haile Selassie and emperors who ruled earlier, the Church, the Imperial family (which itself was said to own some 42 percent of the total land in the state), and the landed class made up a polity that competed structurally. Tenants at the mercy of landlords responded politically to them, while peasants on Church land were completely at its mercy. The Church and the landed class were competing "governments" absorbing whatever surplus income was extracted from the land. The Imperial Office and the individuals who filled the political structures in parliament were also property owners free from land taxes and able to tax tenants. The government, to function financially, had to compete with the Church, the Imperial household, and landlords in terms of taxation. Therefore the tenant farmer was seen as the only taxable entity in a political system made up of an oppressor class unwilling to make any financial sacrifices. The peasant, prior to and under the regime of Haile Selassie, bore the brunt of supporting financially four layers of government: the landed elite, the Church, the central government, and the Imperial family. In this structure the peasant might easily be compared to a serf. Oppressed without mercy he was lucky to survive from year to year. No leader even came close to fundamentally altering the feudal structure, and in fact emperors usually supported it, since it was the determining factor in the accumulation of power and class. Tinkering with feudalism was seen as treasonous and would promptly bring about unified opposition among the traditional forces whose power was seen as threatened. As in the case of Theodore II, who tried to curtail

the Church's land tax rights, it could even lead to the overthrow of an emperor. Feudalism was without question the
political and economic context within which all emperors had
to operate if they wanted to survive.

    When I first traveled through Ethiopia in 1967 I was struck
by stark contrasts. The country has physical beauty of such
extraordinary majesty, particularly in the mountains of the
North. The geographical diversity offers lovely vistas in the
desert, near the Red Sea, and among the many lovely and lazy
lakes that dot the countryside. Ethiopia is simply quite beautiful. At the same time the awfulness of the feudal system left one
amazed and thunderstruck. It seemed incredible that such a
system could exist in the twentieth century. At that time far less
was known about feudalism in Ethiopia and it came as a shock
to learn about all its horrors through doing research on the
subject. It was an anomaly not only within the context of the
twentieth century but also within the realm of Ethiopia's land-
scape. The class system it created, the stratification within it,
and the vigor with which it was defended by the ruling class
throughout Ethiopia's history rubbed against the grain of
Ethiopia's beauty and its lively imperial and mythical history.
Ethiopia was clearly a host of contradictions.

    The elements that make up the contradictions—geography,
history, culture, feudalism—need to be understood, even in a
minor way, if one is to come to grips with the reign and person
of Haile Selassie. For rather than viewing him in a vacuum
one can place him within the context of time and place and
thus better comprehend the forces that made him function as
he did, both personally and politically. Haile Selassie was not
only a man of his time, but more than anything he was a man of
the past, circumscribed by cultural and historical patterns that
he played no part in creating but which determined the
framework through which he had to operate.

3. Prologue: September 12, 1974

It all ended in the cold and the rain.

The rains had drenched Addis Ababa for the past week and the air was cold and damp. The people of the city were awaiting the end of the rains and the first glimmer of sunlight and accompanying warmth. For the past three weeks Haile Selassie, emperor of Ethiopia since 1930 and the only real power in the country since 1916, had not emerged from Jubilee Palace in the modern downtown district of Addis Ababa. Under constant verbal attack for the past year by sections of the Ethiopian military and observing the arrests of almost all members of his personal and governmental entourage, Haile Selassie chose to avoid street disturbances and to some degree exile himself to his palace. Cruel irony for the man who had wielded such authority over Ethiopia and who was regarded as the most authoritative and powerful monarch the country had ever known.

On this day he must have known the end was near. The previous evening the emperor was bitterly attacked on national television for remaining aloof while starvation ran rampant throughout the state. His favorite daughter and closest advisor, Princess Tenegne Work, had been arrested earlier that day. Now no one close to the emperor was left. He was all alone. Peering out of his bedroom window he could see troops on the palace grounds. But rather than guarding him from outsiders, they were keeping him under surveillance. During the past six decades he had modernized and liberalized Ethiopia, had brought it constitutional government, had thrust

himself into the international limelight; when under attack by
Italy in 1936 he had raised on behalf of Ethiopia the issue of
collective security before the League of Nations, and had seen
to it that the Organization of African Unity established its
headquarters in Addis Ababa. But today was a different story.
He was powerless.

Early in the day he was told to prepare himself for an
audience with an official military delegation. A few hours
later, meticulously attired in his heavily decorated military
uniform, he was officially informed by a lower-ranking military officer that he had been deposed. He was then placed
under arrest. The walk from the audience room to the front of
the palace was longer than usual. There must have been a final
dignified look at the map of Ethiopia in one corner of the
room. Then directly outside the office he could not help but
see the photograph of himself standing next to President John
F. Kennedy in Washington in 1963 hanging next to the paint-
ing of Winston Churchill and Anthony Eden conversing with
him in the 1940s. Down the red-carpeted staircase and into the
front hall he could see past the entrance doors into the garden
where his lions and cheetahs were romping in their cages.

It must have been devastating. This proud, noble man, used
to having his orders followed and being in total control, comfortable with all the major leaders of the twentieth century,
now surrounded by troops and being escorted away from all
the power and authority he knew. Ramrod straight, dignified,
peering into the distance past the horrors of the moment, he
did as he was told. With his cape over his shoulders he walked
outside. There in the driveway was an old blue Volkswagen.
Told to get in, he adamantly refused. How could the emperor,
he thought, get into this car when he was accustomed to solid
gold horse-drawn carriages, Rolls Royces and Mercedes-
Benzes? The symbols of monarchy must be retained. But
choice was no longer an option. At gunpoint he placed his
five-foot-four-inch frame into the back of the car and sat as
erect as ever. The humiliation was staggering. But more
shocks were to come. He was taken to army headquarters in
Addis Ababa and placed in squalid surroundings. During the
short drive to the army barracks, the Provisional Military Administrative Committee (Dergue) announced that, "As from

today . . . His Imperial Majesty Haile Selassie has been deposed from office. Haile Selassie I has vacated the National Palace and has been taken to a place prepared for him."[1] A few weeks later he was quartered in one of his palaces outside the capital, and within some months he was returned to Jubilee Palace to live out his days in a small apartment under house arrest.

From the Volkswagen, the now former emperor saw crowds of people yelling "thief" and raising clenched fists at him. The populace was clearly responding to the accusations that Haile Selassie had stolen over a billion dollars from the treasury and had forwarded the money to Switzerland. But the emperor was not thinking of those charges. His thoughts turned to a time when people bowed down as his car passed by, when they prostrated themselves and kissed his feet as he walked among them distributing money and food. When the car turned left onto Menelik I Avenue he could glimpse Africa Hall, the site of meetings of the Organization of African Unity. His thoughts turned to the times he had chaired those meetings and negotiated with African leaders. With a placid but sad smile on his face, the former monarch must have known that were he still wielding authority over his subjects, those violent screams of anger would instead be deferential bows.

As the Volkswagen moved inexorably toward the square, army personnel at the barracks were preparing for the awkward moment of the former emperor's arrival. As the car pulled into the entrance Haile Selassie too was aware of the moment. Fearful of appearing reduced to a lower position in the eyes of his subjects, the once-monarch steeled himself against heartbreak and humiliation. Smartly stepping from the car he walked briskly past the soldiers and into the barracks. He did not so much as look into the eyes of his guards. Once inside he was taken to a filthy room and left alone with his thoughts.

Tanks, armored cars, and jeeps crowded with soldiers manned key points in the capital. Despite the constant drizzle and cold, Ethiopians in Addis Ababa gathered to talk about the overthrow. Although the deposition had been expected, its arrival was stunning. Troops forced people from the streets, all except those hurling insults at the emperor and praising the

action of the military. In the bars and drinking parlors, in res-
taurants and hotels, and in the privacy of homes the ouster of
the emperor was the sole topic of discussion. Many wondered if
he could retake his throne. But the reign of Haile Selassie I was
over. Never again would this world figure attain power. Alone in
the military barracks, he must have known this. There was no
power, there were few allies who were not dead, in prison or in
exile. Haile Selassie was alone as never before and he knew it.
He had lost the power and control he so cherished and needed.

In 1972, when the emperor turned eighty, many Ethiopians
and foreigners hoped he would take the occasion to freely
relinquish the throne and turn power over to his son Asfa
Wossen. The crown prince, at that time aged fifty-six, was
considered by Ethiopians as weak and certainly no replace-
ment for his father. Still, the fear was that should the emperor
not relinquish authority peacefully, he might be turned out
violently at some future time. In 1967 the crown prince stated
in an interview that, upon his succession to the throne, he
would liberalize Ethiopia, move quickly for land reform programs, and would do what he could to better the fortunes of
the peasantry in the country.[2] But Haile Selassie did not relinquish the throne. Instead he tried to hold on as long as he could.

On this Thursday morning Haile Selassie did lose power. It
was neither voluntary nor peaceful. And within the next four
years Ethiopia was to see more internal turmoil than it had
witnessed in decades.

The rains continued throughout the day and people did
what they could to protect themselves from the penetrating
cold. Haile Selassie, wrapped in his cape, eating army
provisions, and being humbled as never before, could
only wonder what forces were at work to bring him to
this ignoble end. His Imperial Majesty, The Conquering Lion of the Tribe of Judah, Elect of God, King of Kings,
Emperor of Ethiopia, the man who had wielded absolute
power longer than any other head of state, had been de-
throned.

As evening approached, the temperature fell near 40°F, but
with the rain and dampness it felt much colder in Addis
Ababa. And as this day was ending so too was an era. The

pomp and circumstance that surrounded the emperor was not with him this night as he, along with others in Addis Ababa, fought to ward off the cold. Alone in his barren room with soldiers stationed just outside the door he ended his evening with his usual prayers. The stoic emperor concluded his final day in office cold, alone, lonely, and politically impotent.

4. The Struggle to Survive

Haile Selassie, which literally means *Might of the Trinity*, was the name Tafari Makonnen adopted upon becoming emperor in 1930. It is the name that history permanently pinned to him and by which he is known throughout the world. For most of us a name is merely a label chosen by others that serves to identify the individual. But the name Haile Selassie was carefully selected by Tafari Makonnen to serve as a symbol for a man who believed in and wanted others to accept the power, authority and legitimacy of his rule. The avenue to power, however, was strewn with personal and political obstacles that became evident during Tafari Makonnen's early life.

Born July 23, 1892, some eighteen miles northeast of the town of Harar, his existence appeared to begin with all the advantages inherent in being born into a family of upper-class heritage. His father, *Ras* (Prince) Makonnen, was the great-grandson of King Sahle Selassie, the nineteenth-century Shoan ruler who had forced the Galla to accept his authority, and was also cousin, friend, close ally of and potential successor to Emperor Menelik II who was then on the throne. *Ras* Makonnen was, at the time, governor of Harar, one of the more important Ethiopian provinces, to which he had been appointed in 1879. Totally faithful to Menelik, the elder Makonnen fought with the emperor against the Italians who tried without success to occupy the country in 1896, and served as Menelik's unofficial minister of foreign affairs, there being at the time no official ministerial structure.

23

Tafari Makonnen's mother, Wayzaro Yashimabet, who was
of Galla descent, died only two years after his birth. The most
powerful but contradictory influence upon Tafari was his
father. In almost the sole emotional description in his autobiography, Haile Selassie recalled the relationship between
the two. "As the love that existed between . . . my father and
myself was altogether special I can feel it up to the present
[1937]. He always used to praise me for the work which I was
doing and for my being obedient. His officers and men used to
love me respectfully because they observed with admiration
the affection which my father had for me."[1] For one who rarely
displayed any emotion whatsoever these were strong words
indeed and they were clear indications of a bond that seemed
to exist between father and son. "As I grew up," Haile Selassie
continued, "the spiritual desire was guiding me to emulate
him and so to conduct myself that his example should dwell
within me."[2]

Appearing much younger than his years, *Ras* Makonnen was
a strikingly good-looking man whose household was a mix of
European and Shoan-Amharic culture. Having traveled
abroad often, including one journey that took him to the coronation of Edward VII of England, *Ras* Makonnen, who had
been granted the title *ras* (prince) in 1890, was convinced of
the importance of European education both on a personal and
on a political level. Along with Menelik, Makonnen strongly
believed that Ethiopia had much to learn from Europe and
such knowledge could clearly aid in the development of the
country away from its feudal and economically undeveloped
state. Since "my father had a strong desire to see the people
get accustomed to the work of civilization which he had observed in Europe"[3] he arranged that a Dr. Vitalien, a French
citizen from Guadeloupe, be brought into the house to teach
French to the ten-year-old Tafari and his cousin, the future
Ras Imru. The work of Vitalien was soon reinforced by Abba
Samuel, an Ethiopian attached to the French mission, whom
Tafari revered as a man who showered him with the personal
attention his own father never displayed.

Thus elements of European modernization via the French
language and Western education were incorporated into the
home of *Ras* Makonnen, while at the same time the traditional

values associated with being a descendant of the Shoan aristocracy were assimilated by Tafari Makonnen. The opposing strains in these two cultures—the one based on liberal democracy and the other on a feudal hierarchy totally undemocratic in nature—must have been quite confusing to Tafari, a confusion that became evident to observers after 1930 when the emperor found it impossible to accommodate the demands of both cultures with one and then the other pushing him in completely different political directions. But for now Tafari acquired the rudiments of a European education, an unusual occurrence for the son of a nobleman. How unusual was made clear by Menelik himself shortly after the death of *Ras* Makonnen in 1906. When Menelik opened a school for Ethiopians to study foreign languages, Tafari was not included among the students. When he tentatively approached Menelik to ask why, he was told by the monarch, "It is because you were a governor [recently appointed] that I thought you chose to live like the nobles, but if you wish to study, then go and learn."[4]

Despite European influences *Ras* Makonnen patterned his house along the lines demanded of an Amharic nobleman. With a personal military of more than six thousand men, and owning a huge amount of tax-free land partly inherited and partly bestowed upon him by Menelik, *Ras* Makonnen was a classic example of the old nobility who represented the pinnacle of status and class in Ethiopia. The Makonnen house was based upon the model established in the imperial court. "In general, the Abyssinian noble attempted to behave like a king in his own sphere of influence and to reproduce in his own court that of the emperor."[5] Masses of retainers and servants met the personal needs of all members of the family, the army was used to ensure the payment of rent and taxes by tenant farmers and to secure the property from the armies of other noblemen, and in the case of *Ras* Makonnen the governor attended to his official duties that included judging cases of litigation in the court of Harar.

Everyday existence was based upon the fealty and deference of one's inferiors, including children, inside the household and out. Rich and privileged far beyond the means of almost the entire population, the Shoan nobility that claimed

descent from the Solomonic dynasty were both feared and
honored, particularly by the peasants and tenant farmers living within their domain. During Menelik's reign, one traveler
detailed other benefits afforded men of noble rank.

> The wealthier men wear a black cloak of silk or bombazine, which
> looks smarter. The men affect Italian hats to a great extent. In wet
> weather . . . there is a black cloak of wool, with a cowl for the head,
> and keeps the wearer beautifully dry and warm. The better class wear
> a sword, often with a silver inlaid sheath, while an attendant carries
> their rifle in front. Round the waist a bandolier of cartridges is always
> worn, and sometimes a revolver or pistol. It is beneath anybody of
> any consequence to walk on foot for even a few yards, and to cover
> the shortest distances a mule is saddled.[6]

According to Levine, the social space of a nobleman is
crowded with issuing orders, to his own servants and to those
of others, while the male heirs are patiently taught the virtues
of obedience and the art of manipulation.[7] Above all, the old
nobility viewed themselves as the carriers of a traditional and
vibrant culture into which their children must be socialized
and which all Ethiopians of lesser birth must respect and fear.
They were the elite class of Ethiopia; they made the political
decisions, set the cultural standards, and sent their armies to
defend the state. They attempted to live as the emperor lived,
though on a lesser scale, and demanded the same allegiance
from their serfs and personal retainers. Wherever the nobleman went, peasants prostrated themselves and servants scur-
ried about doing all they could to attend to his pleasure.

In 1967 the provincial governor of Gojam, Tsehai Inqu
Selassie, invited me, along with some others, to a breakfast at
his home. At what could not have been so very different from
what might have occurred in the nineteenth century, hordes of
servants went scurrying about serving goat meat, the traditional Ethiopian dish *injara* and *wat*, raw beef, and gallons
of Ethiopian honey-wine known as *tajj*, all the while behaving
with the utmost docility and servility that seemed to demand
of them a polite bow each time they neared our table. The
attention paid to us, however, was nothing next to the fuss
and bother that was generated by the governor's presence. All
this activity was part of ruling class culture, and *Ras* Makonnen was very much a part and representation of this element of
Ethiopia.

Thus, the first decade of Tafari Makonnen's life saw an intermingling of European and Shoan-Amhara culture imposed upon him. Trained in the French language, having French-speaking tutors, and becoming acquainted with the rudiments of European society, he was socialized to accept the values of a modern Western culture. At the same time he was reared in large part by his maternal grandmother, Wayzaro Wallata Giyorgis, who, together with the aristocratic Amhara culture that so surrounded him in the home, prepared him to expect that the benefits of status and class represented by his father should devolve upon him. He was trained within the context of two cultures but there can be no doubt that the indigenous strain was far more influential since it had greater immediate impact through the vitality of an everyday presence.

Most important, Haile Selassie's formative years were a complex amalgam of emotional contradictions. Tafari was functionally motherless and without question felt abandoned by her.[8] He was angry at her for dying, for leaving him alone to contend with the varied forces of life. Although this was clearly outside his own awareness at the time, he was quietly furious. In his writings Haile Selassie never mentions his mother except in passing, and never once describes any emotional feeling toward her. His grandmother did not fill the vacuum created by the death of her daughter. This became clear much later in Tafari's life when he directed much of his fury at two women who at one point had a great amount of control over him: Menelik's wife and daughter Empress Taitu and Empress Zauditu. When Tafari felt certain of his authority over them, he went after them with a vengeance and is said to have had a hand in the death of Zauditu.[9] Had the grandmother served as an adequate substitute for the mother there would not have been rancor of such deep-seatedness directed at these women in particular.

Ras Makonnen tried to give his son a great deal of love and security. Between the time of his mother's death in 1894 and Ras Makonnen's demise in 1906, Tafari Makonnen was given some emotional support by his father. The words by which Tafari recalls his father are laced with love and affection and give credence to the hypothesis that Ras Makonnen was a

good father who tried, insofar as was possible, to substitute for
the mother. But this support had its constrictive features. *Ras*
Makonnen was an extremely busy man who often visited
Addis Ababa to proclaim his own fealty to Menelik, and
traveled abroad often on behalf of the emperor, and who, in
his own capacity as governor of Harar, had varied responsibilities that often took him away from home. In addition,
Amhara culture demanded a strict hierarchy of roles that emphasized, for the father, responsibility rather than physical
affection.[10] Within Amhara culture it was virtually impossible
for *Ras* Makonnen to play his role as father any differently. He
was a man firmly embedded in his culture and although Tafari
obviously understood this and was sympathetic he did not
hold his father entirely blameless. In part, Abba Samuel
served as substitute father, and Tafari's relationship with his
father was extremely contradictory.

Tafari Makonnen loved his father, a point that is evident in
his autobiography. But the death of *Ras* Makonnen in 1906,
when Tafari was merely fourteen years old, once again
brought out feelings of abandonment. Within twelve years
Tafari's ego had been crushed twice, upon the death of each of
his parents. No longer the center of anyone's universe, Tafari,
the sole surviving child of his parents' marriage, felt completely deprived, and no longer in real control of the world
around him. The death of his father must have caused immense suffering. It "had deprived him of protection while his
genealogical credentials made him suspect to the major contenders for the succession" to the throne.[11] Tafari had to learn
to rely totally upon his own resources. Though he spoke affec-
tionately of his father, Tafari's words are so laden with emotion and so different in style from anything else Haile Selassie
ever wrote that there had to be meaning in those words far
beyond the apparent. Never, at least on paper, did Tafari ever
convey such emotion, over any single individual either before
or after he became emperor. Traumatized and alone, Tafari at
some point created the myth of the extraordinary father, in
large part, as a reaction-formation to the reality of the situation.
Feeling as abandoned by his father as by his mother but
recognizing that his father tried to bestow love upon him,
Tafari loved him intellectually and hated him emotionally. No

matter how much his father tried to substitute for his mother and no matter how much a prisoner he was to his culture he had, in fact, in Tafari's mind, betrayed him by leaving him so alone and, upon his death, helpless. Thus there were love and hate and Tafari's words about his father represent both emotions. Clearly unaware of the meaning of all of this, Tafari believed strongly that he loved his father, believed that his father had cared for him by bringing in French tutors, and had shown his trust in him by appointing him in 1905 *Dejaz-match* (Keeper of the Door, a largely honorary title) of a region of Harar Province. Love and hate, affection and abandonment were incompatible traits that Tafari Makonnen associated with his father; hate and abandonment were the characteristics he applied to his mother.

The years 1892–1906 were of prime importance to the emotional makeup of the future emperor. Essentially deprived of love and security by the loss of his mother, and after the death of his father harassed by claimants to the throne, Tafari Makonnen had to spend these and future years desperately attempting to exert some control and security over his own life. That meant, in the milieu in which he existed, that he would have to become emperor—no other position would afford him total security and control. Ensuring control meant dominance over all others in Ethiopia and no other political position but emperor would offer Tafari Makonnen the security he so needed. Fortunately, he lived within the proper genealogical galaxy through which this goal could be reached. Besieged by European and Amharic influences, Tafari would forever be confused as to the relevance of each vis-à-vis his own power. Functionally he learned to use for his own purposes whatever cultural trait offered him the most emotional and political security. But he was caught between both cultures and had to figure out where he *wanted* to position himself culturally as opposed to where he *needed* to because of political expediency.

These years were critical but complex. Tafari Makonnen existed without emotional or cultural security and this caused him to seek both with driving passion. If security is the parent of contentment and happiness then Tafari Makonnen at this stage in his life was fatherless and childless. But he had every intention, whether he knew it or not, of filling the vacuum of security by exerting absolute control over all others. Only in this way could security be restored to him. But he had to bide his time and in the process he would become a master of manipulation relying on his own resources in order to ward off danger whenever it approached. Whatever anger he felt had to be kept private; Amhara culture disallowed its display,[12] and permitting its emergence would have provoked his enemies.

The years following *Ras* Makonnen's death were difficult ones for Tafari. Hopeful of replacing his father as governor of Harar, the teenage Tafari was both angry and crushed when the position was awarded to his half brother by Menelik II. Tafari believed that he was the legitimate heir as he was the son of *Ras* Makonnen's most recent marriage. Yelma Makonnen was the only son born to *Ras* Makonnen and his first wife, Wayzaro Assallafatch, the daughter of Empress Taitu's sister. Menelik's present wife, Empress Taitu, insisted that Yelma be appointed to the prestigious position at Harar, while she also made sure that Tafari would be granted a position of far lesser importance. Fearful that Tafari's lineage would eventually carry him to the imperial throne Taitu did what she could to ensure that the monarchy would remain in the hands of her own family. Tafari, who was rapidly learning the art of silence, claimed that he never wanted the position but that all his father's friends and military supporters strongly believed the governorship should be awarded to him as he had a more equitable claim to the position than did his half brother. This was obviously his own belief, spoken through his advocates. Tafari was furious at the empress and in his autobiography allowed his opinion and anger subtle expression. "Empress Taitu, used to supporting all her relatives, was said to be exerting herself with a view to Dejazmatch Yelma getting the governorship of Harar, arguing that, while there is an elder son, the younger son should not be appointed. . . . Since . . . Empress Taitu had pestered Emperor Menelik . . . the matter was decided."[13]

Tafari refused to blame Menelik for not bestowing the governorship upon him, but placed all responsibility upon Taitu. The word *pestered* in his description of the circumstances surrounding the appointment indicated his feelings since it was never used again in the entire autobiography and was a word alien to the emperor's general pattern of speech. For the first time since his father's death Tafari Makonnen felt the ire of one who mistrusted him, and the helplessness that came from being unable to exert any control over her. In 1906, in an attempt to assuage Tafari, Empress Taitu had him appointed governor of a tiny and unimportant region northwest of Addis Ababa known as Selale. But it was a meaningless appointment because *Ras* Makonnen's lands and the bulk of his army went to Tafari's half brother and Tafari himself was left powerless. The position was held in absentia as the youthful Tafari was forced by Taitu to remain in Menelik's palace so that he could be watched. "For the next [two] years [he] lived in Menelik's palace where he received a thorough education in all the intricate aspects of the art of power manipulation. Menelik's court seethed with intrigue as the struggle for succession unfolded."[14]

Tafari's political and personal insecurity increased markedly immediately after his appointment. Menelik II became gravely ill in 1906 and two years later he was hit with a stroke that left him fully paralyzed until his death in December 1913. With Menelik unable to exert power or authority, his palace became the center of a series of plots wherein various groups were positioning themselves to eventually grab the throne. With no army to speak of, Tafari's very existence was threatened, and to stay alive in this seething atmosphere he had to sharpen his manipulative skills so as to convince the various contenders to the throne that he had no interest in becoming emperor. With Menelik ill, all the work of government was taken over by Empress Taitu, and as Tafari cunningly put it, "peace became disturbed."[15] Tafari was constantly besieged with demands that he join one group of conspirators or another, but he was careful, knowing that Taitu was looking for a chance to get rid of him, and thus he refused at that time to participate in any action that might threaten his position.

The emotional situation confronting Tafari was extraordinarily complex. Menelik had been a supporter of Tafari and was extremely fond of him. His incapacity forced Tafari to link Menelik emotionally with his father, *Ras* Makonnen. Menelik

was seen by Tafari as abandoning him much like his father
had, leaving him at the mercy of all the contending forces in
the palace. Though Tafari respected and revered Menelik he
could not help but feel that this last of his protectors was, by
his illness, leaving him completely helpless, and thus the
same feelings of anger that arose upon the deaths of his parents once again made themselves apparent. The love/hate
duality that Tafari felt about his father was projected by Tafari
upon Menelik. The three people he had loved and revered
most, and who were able to offer him protection—his mother,
father, and the emperor—had abandoned him, and in so doing,
had thrust him into a position of total insecurity. He was
unable to exert any control and was now under the influence
of a woman, Empress Taitu, who had made it clear to him from
the very beginning that she viewed him as a threat and was out
to destroy him. With no influential support left, Tafari was
thrown upon his own resources that had to be honed to utter
perfection were he to survive. He must have been furious with
Menelik, but once again rather than take his anger out upon a
man, he would soon direct it at Taitu who served as the image
of that person whose neglect through abandonment had been
the most traumatic for Tafari—his mother.

Now in almost full control of the monarchy, Empress Taitu
decided to position Tafari Makonnen away from the palace,
thereby removing him from proximity to the levers of power.
In 1908 she had Tafari appointed to the governorship of a
portion of Sidamo Province, the southernmost area of
Ethiopia. With his grandmother, Wayzaro Wallata Giyorgis,
and three thousand men of his father's army, he proceeded to
Sidamo. Exercising his judicial and administrative responsibilities free of the anxiety that was always present in him at
the palace, Tafari "had a time of perfect joy [and] encountered
no trouble whatever."[16]

From 1908 to 1910 Tafari ruled Sidamo while in Addis
Ababa plots were swirling all around Taitu. Fearful that
Menelik might recover and discover their activities but even
more afraid of Taitu's attempts to permanently install her own
family upon the throne, various princes (*rases*) were conspir-
ing to remove her from power. In 1907 Menelik had announced that his grandson Lij Yasu, then a boy of twelve, was

to be his successor. A wild and independent child who always went his own way, he would have been impossible for Taitu to influence. After Menelik's stroke in 1908 she exerted all her authority in an attempt to have Zauditu, Menelik's daughter by an earlier wife, replace Lij Yasu as heir to the throne, and to have herself declared regent by the Church, thus becoming the true and legitimate source of power in Ethiopia. Empress Taitu was Menelik's fourth wife and he her fifth husband. She had always played a role in her husband's decisions and was comfortable with power and decision-making. Believing that she could easily control Zauditu, she refused to acknowledge Lij Yasu's claim to the throne. *Ras* Tasamma, who was regent, having been appointed to the position by Menelik, opposed Taitu's now blatant attempts to place members of her own family in positions of authority; between 1908 and 1910 *Ras* Tasamma and Empress Taitu were engaged in a deadly struggle, both vying for control of the throne.

In 1908 Tafari's half brother died and the post of governor of Harar became vacant. From 1908 to 1910 it was granted to one of Menelik's military commanders who was supported by the empress. Tafari, who had every right to the position, was kept from it through influence exerted upon Menelik by Taitu. In 1910, however, *Ras* Tasamma, with the support of some powerful *rases*, forced the empress to appoint Tafari to the position, and in March it was granted to him. Tafari was merely a tool used by *Ras* Tasamma to delimit some of the power of the empress, and even though Tafari was pleased with the appointment, he knew that his position was tentative and based completely upon the good will of *Ras* Tasamma.

Shortly after his appointment Tafari joined with *Ras* Tasamma, *Ras* Bitwaddad Mangasha Atikam, *Fitwarari* (General) Habte Giorgis, and others, to remove Taitu from the seat of power. With their militaries surrounding the palace, they informed the empress that she must "reside in the Palace and look after the sick Emperor . . . but the work of government she should leave to the regent *Ras* Bitwaddad Tasamma."[17] Thus a coup had been effected, and in the process Tafari Makonnen, who knew that his own position depended totally upon *Ras* Tasamma, had helped to destroy Empress Taitu. Although he secured his political position, this was also the first time the anger felt toward his mother found any release. The empress was seen by Tafari as a mother image, and aiding in her removal allowed Tafari to release the fury that had been pent up inside since his mother's abandonment of him upon her death.

By appearing to support *Ras* Tasamma, Tafari had manipulated himself into a stronger position politically than he had known in years. Although Empress Taitu, who had done all she could to destroy Tafari and the Makonnen house, was now out of the way, he was still totally dependent upon the good graces of *Ras* Tasamma. The removal of the empress was a major political and personal victory for Tafari and would always retain its sweetness since it was the first time since his father's death that such success had been achieved by him.

With the bulk of *Ras* Makonnen's army restored to him, Tafari went to Harar in 1910 and proceeded to build a personal following loyal to him. Easing the exploitation visited upon his subjects by the two previous governors, he revamped the administrative system, reduced the amount of land taxes to be paid by tenant farmers, and ended the use of forced labor. He thereby generated a large amount of support from his people. At the same time he developed his army, securing for them the arms that were necessary for the battle for power that was sure to come. It came soon. In 1911 *Ras* Tasamma died and Menelik's council of ministers declared that the sixteen-year-old Lij Yasu was old enough to act for himself. Another struggle for power ensued while Menelik II continued to languish in the total incapacity in which his stroke had left him.

The same year, 1911, Tafari Makonnen married Woizero Menen, a deeply religious Galla of Wello Province who believed firmly in the tenets of the Ethiopian Orthodox Church. A niece of Lij Yasu, she was forced by him to marry Tafari who was himself ordered to leave his first wife. In this way Lij Yasu hoped to neutralize Tafari as a threat. As a member of the ruling family, Tafari might not opt for achieving the throne himself. But this action had just the opposite effect on Tafari. It was an indication of how little control he had over his own life and it only reinforced in him the desire to control absolutely all aspects of his existence. Only the throne could offer him this control and he was more adamant than ever that he would have to become emperor.

In 1913 Menelik finally died. Because of fears of a wide-spread civil war revolving around the throne, his death was kept generally secret and Lij Yasu remained uncrowned, although in fact he was now emperor. The old nobility who had been reduced in power by Menelik and who had been thwarted in their attempt to take power by Taitu, moved quickly to secure their positions. Unified in their resistance to Lij Yasu because of his opposition to them, his renunciation of Christianity and his conversion to Islam, the Shoan nobles closed ranks against him. With the support of the Ethiopian Orthodox Church in 1916, they proclaimed Menelik's daughter Zauditu empress and on February 11, 1917, she was crowned. Lij Yasu was excommunicated by the Church which together with the new government sought Lij Yasu's imprisonment. Lij Yasu fled into the interior to raise an army. Tafari Makonnen, who supported the *rases* and the Church, was made regent and heir presumptive, obtaining the title *ras*, while *Fitwarari* Habte Giorgis became minister of war. "In the new situation Tafari represented modernist influences, the Empress a vague and uncertain middle ground, and the war minister, along with the [Church], the forces of tradition."[18]

Lij Yasu's acceptance of Islam had posed the most fundamental threat to the Shoan nobles. It served as the clearest indication that Lij Yasu, with Muslim support, would overthrow the Solomonic line that had been in power for centuries. Christianity in Ethiopia was also threatened. A major economic and political institution since the fourth century, the Ethiopian Orthodox Church was unwilling to see its position in the Ethiopian ruling order altered. Tafari, who had been personally abused by Lij Yasu through his forced marriage, and who was unwilling to see his climb to absolute power stymied by an emperor who, being young, might rule for ages, supported the old nobility with all the force that his army represented. Believing they could control the twenty-five-year-old, the war lords placed Tafari in the position of regent. Thus began a thirteen-year power struggle that would see *Ras* Tafari Makonnen pitted against Habte Giorgis and Empress Zauditu. Along the way *Ras* Tafari would have to contend with a multiplicity of political figures who periodically emerged as threats to his political position. "The three leading figures at court . . . at once began to fence for position. They were

almost equally matched in influence and following, and no
one of them succeeded in gaining a marked advantage until
death removed [Habte Giorgis] in 1926."[19]

The influence of *Ras* Makonnen upon his son became evident at once. Tafari was intent on modernizing and Westerniz-
ing Ethiopia. In 1920 he had administrative regulations and
code books shipped from various European countries which
were used as models by which to begin an Ethiopian bureaucracy. Ministers were appointed to advise the regent and for the
first time were housed in their own official accommodations in
Addis Ababa. Electricity came to Ethiopia in 1922 and in the
same year automobiles were imported for use by the palace
and the old elite. In 1923 Ethiopia was accepted as a member
of the League of Nations upon the initiative of *Ras* Tafari. One
year later Tafari traveled to Europe for the first time, accompanied by six lions, four zebras, and thirty personal attendants.
Much was achieved during the course of the trip which took
him to France, Belgium, Italy, Great Britain, and Greece.
Europeans, influenced by the regent, came to Ethiopia to
assist in the modernization of the country and to advise Tafari
regarding plans he had in mind. Ethiopia was granted port
facilities in Assab in the Italian colony of Eritrea that permitted Ethiopia to escape from its landlocked position. Intro-
duced to the benefits of Westernization by his father, Tafari
wasted little time in procuring help from Europe. In 1924 *Ras*
Tafari abolished slavery. The impact of his Western education
was thus seen immediately upon his designation as regent.

While *Ras* Tafari engineered the Westernization of Ethiopia,
he had all the while to contend with his domestic opposition.
Owning upwards of four million acres of land, Habte Giorgis
had no intention of seeing the regent ruin the feudal base
upon which Ethiopia was built. Allied with the empress and
elements of the nobility, he fought desperately to reduce
Tafari's power. Tafari, on the other hand, knew that to defeat
his two rivals he needed the support of the landed nobility and
thus he had no intention of causing the erosion of the feudal
structure. Together with his friend and ally *Ras* Kassa the
regent went about trying to secure support from the numerous
and powerful *rases*. Although he believed that Empress
Zauditu showed him almost a "mother's regard,"[20] he was

convinced that because of pressure placed upon her by priests and conservative noblemen that she was out to strip him of his power. The regent therefore had to be extraordinarily careful. It was vital that he know at all times what the plans of his two major enemies were, and through the careful placement of informants this became possible.

In 1921 the one person who was able to unite *Ras* Tafari, Empress Zauditu, and Habte Giorgis—Lij Yasu—was finally captured, and imprisoned in gold chains. Although the capture was a victory for the triumvirate and stabilized the positions of all three, it also served to aggravate the antagonisms among them since no unifying force existed any longer that could pull them together. For the next five years each attempted to out-maneuver the other. The deadlock was broken in 1926 when Habte Giorgis died of natural causes.

It was now the regent against the empress with each desperately trying to outwit the other. Tafari, however, viewed Zauditu through two lenses, one political and the other personal. Although he was out to defeat her so as to finally attain the position of emperor, he was also out to get her as she was the living personification of his mother who had emotionally ruined him by leaving him completely helpless. It is no accident that Tafari referred to Zauditu as mother[21] because that is exactly how he pictured her. She mirrored his mother because both tried to destroy him and both represented forces that threw him to the wind. His mother had hurt him desperately and Zauditu was trying to do the same. He was fearful that Zauditu, should she be victorious over him in the struggle for the crown, would force him to do her bidding and thus he would be out of control, his life at her mercy. This, above all, must not happen. He could never face the anxiety that he felt at being so out of control when first his mother and then his father died. He thus moved with incredible speed to gain the upper hand over Zauditu and to rally all the forces that he could muster against her.

Tafari acquired the 16,000 personal troops and all the lands of Habte Giorgis, moved at once to banish the leading religious supporter of the empress, and sent his troops to defeat *Dejazmatch* Balcha of Sidamo, a leading figure in the nobility and a supporter of Zauditu. Habte Giorgis's properties were

distributed to noblemen sympathetic to the regent and to
those marginal in their allegiance, and each was granted the
right to tax the peasants working the land. Through the use of
patronage Tafari Makonnen absorbed the political support and
the armies of the nobility. Zauditu was pushed further and
further into a corner while Tafari exerted more and more
authority. In 1928 he forced the empress to crown him *negus*
(king), threatening to forcibly remove her from the throne
should she refuse. In early 1930 Zauditu struck back. Her
husband *Ras* Gugsa Wolie mobilized his army and marched
against the regent. Tafari sent his army to confront him; *Ras*
Gugsa was killed and his army defeated. Two days later, on
April 2, 1930, Empress Zauditu died under the most mysterious of circumstances, and *Ras* Tafari became emperor of
Ethiopia though his official coronation would not take place
until November. The struggle for succession ended seventeen
years after the death of Menelik II.

Until 1930 *Ras* Tafari Makonnen's life was made up of a
series of traumas. The premature deaths of his parents and
Menelik's disability generated emotional anxiety and insecurity because Tafari was left alone to deal with forces he found
hazardous. Lonely, out of control, hungry for love, he was
forced to forego the liveliness and happiness of a well-to-do
youth, concentrating on preserving his existence. Tafari's
capacity to think and act outside of his self-interest was piti-
fully limited.[22] This was reinforced by the reality of a situation
where others were out to destroy him, and by the emphasis in
Amhara experience and culture on the personal ego where the
self is viewed as the center of society.[23] Thus Tafari emerged
from childhood emotionally crippled, in need of love but unable to attain it, young but youthless, abandoned and longing
for control, and with an ego that had been stunted at two and
crushed thereafter. Where most people spend years developing their fantasies about life and what it will offer to them, *Ras*
Tafari could have no fantasies; if he wanted to survive he had
to direct himself solely to the attainment of the monarchy.
Responsibility came early, disallowing him the luxury of
frivolousness. Robbed of the security of normal development
that leads to a sense of personal ability to control, he had to
reach the position of total dominance over all others in order to
achieve emotional and physical security. When his childhood

tutor and companion Abba Samuel drowned in 1915 Tafari lost "the last person he ever completely trusted."[24] In 1894, when he was two, his mother died; in 1906 he lost his father; two years later Menelik II became so ill as to be useless and in 1913 his stroke finally killed him; in 1915 his only true friend in life, Abba Samuel, died in a freak accident. These emotional shocks without question wreaked havoc upon *Ras* Tafari and throughout his life he tried to compensate for his emotionally shrivelled state.

In addition to being hurt and feeling thrown to the wind, Tafari was angry. Furious mostly at his mother for abandoning him so suddenly, he projected his rage upon those women in his life who had a certain amount of control over him. Taitu and Zauditu represented his mother and it was upon these two images that Tafari lashed out hardest. His forced marriage only served to complicate his feelings towards women, and also must have reproduced the feeling that attaining a woman's love and emotional support was impossible for him. This too he fully blamed his mother for. When his wife, Empress Menen, died in 1962 Haile Selassie's eulogy of her was absolutely devoid of emotion. "She was religious. . . . We never had differences that needed the intervention of others. . . . As Sarah was to Abraham, so was she obedient to me. Our wishes were mutual. . . . Her assistance for the good of the young, the old and the needy requires no testimony."[25] Although they had three sons and three daughters their life together appeared to lack emotional and physical passion.

Ras Tafari was angry at his father for leaving him so helpless, but this was complicated by an intellectual love that in the final analysis curtailed the intensity of his anger towards men as a group. Although he struggled to destroy all men who stood in his way his activity was motivated as much by political exigencies as by emotional needs, though the latter certainly played a powerful role.

The emotional destruction of *Ras* Tafari served to reinforce the cultural demands placed upon a Shoan-Amhara nobleman. All of Haile Selassie's actions did not stem purely from an emotional void, but his anger was a vital prop that disallowed him from relating to others with care and love. Always severe, his early life convinced him that he could only trust himself. All others he knew would eventually let him down just as his

parents and Menelik did, and perhaps as Abba Samuel did at
his death. This perception was to have a profound impact
upon Haile Selassie's political career, as he would often per-
sonalize the political arena which would disallow him from
making rational, as opposed to subjective, decisions.

Although responsibility is placed on the shoulders of children relatively early in Ethiopia, Tafari never lived without it.
What he did live without was protection, love, warmth, and
security. His whole life was an attempt to achieve these feelings, and the position of emperor would, he thought, afford
him the opportunity. He knew that without this highest of all
positions he would remain insecure and anxious. So he went
after the throne, directing almost the entire first four decades of
his life to acquiring it. It is said that "uneasy lies the head that
wears the crown" but in Tafari Makonnen's case, wearing the
crown was the only way he would ever rest eas y.

After Empress Zauditu's death in April 1930 *Ras* Tafari
Makonnen held the prize in his hands: he was emperor. Security, order, control, protection, were the words he associated
with the crown and he would do all he could to keep himself
emperor.

So as to allow time for all the dignitaries to arrive from
all over the world and to make plans for the celebration, the
official coronation of *Ras* Tafari Makonnen as Emperor Haile
Selassie I was delayed until November 1930. Unlike Lij Yasu,
Tafari Makonnen would be crowned—the first officially
crowned emperor since Menelik II.

The nightmare years were now over and *Ras* Tafari had no
intention whatsoever of being a weak emperor. As one observer noted in 1910, "Succession is not considered of much
account in Abyssinia, and any strong man in the kingdom has a
great chance of obtaining the throne. . . . Menelik himself
. . . took the throne by the sword, and it is quite likely that the
next ruler will not depart from the usual custom in this respect."[26] And now, in 1930, as far as *Ras* Tafari was concerned,
no one would take his throne away from him. He had it and he
would keep it. The coronation in November would only
legitimize what he had attained in April. *Ras* Tafari Makonnen
was emperor of Ethiopia.

5. The Coronation of *Ras* Tafari Makonnen

Addis Ababa was the scene of much confusion and running around during the months of October and November 1930. With the crowning of the emperor due to occur November 2, the ramshackle town was being dressed up for the arrival of foreign guests. Contradictions were everywhere.

> The streets were crowded with sheep, goats, cattle, donkeys, and camels. . . . Through this mass of animals move crowds of men, all carrying guns or swords. A ras . . . rides by on his donkey, followed by his suite running on foot. The bigger the ras, the bigger the retinue. And through these crowds run motor cars, worming their way in and out.[1]

According to Evelyn Waugh,

> The first, obvious, inescapable impression was that nothing was ready or could possibly be made ready in time for the official opening of the celebrations. . . . The whole town seemed still in a rudimentary stage of construction. At every corner were half-finished buildings; some had already been abandoned.
> Down the centre of the main thoroughfares run metalled tracks for motor traffic, bordered on either side by dust and loose stones for mules and pedestrians. The usual way for an Abyssinian gentleman to travel is straight down the middle of the road on mule-back with ten or twenty armed retainers trotting all around him.[2]

Ras Tafari Makonnen had Ethiopia purchase the state coach of Imperial Germany, while coronets with King Solomon's seal and the Lion of Judah incorporated in the motif were being readied in Great Britain. Priests of the Ethiopian Orthodox Church streamed into the city from the provinces, while soldiers paraded daily. Foreign guests arrived via Djibouti where they took special trains from that French colony through the interior of Ethiopia into Addis Ababa. By the end of October all foreign envoys had arrived. Among them were the Duke of Gloucester representing Great Britain, the Prince of Udine who came from Italy, the Greek Count P. Metaxas, Baron H.K.C. Bildt, the envoy from Sweden, Isaburo Yoshida of Japan, Murray Jacob of the United States, and Muhammad Tawfiq Nasim Pasha representing the King of Egypt.

Prior to the coronation, the official celebrations were inaugurated by the unveiling of the Menelik II memorial situated in front of the Cathedral of St. George. It is extraordinarily interesting to look at this ceremony from the viewpoint of two who were present at the occasion as they pointedly show the different political perceptions of that event. *Ras* Tafari curtly but respectfully remembers the occasion in this way:

> We had caused to be set up, in the vicinity of the royal church of St. George, a statue of the great Emperor Menelik II. The work was eventually completed and it was then determined that it should be inaugurated on the eve of the coronation. Consequently, after all the guests who had come for Our coronation had arrived with much ceremonial to be present there at, We made a lengthy speech explaining the propriety of erecting a statue. . . . When We had finished, We gave the honour of uncovering the veil with which the statue had been wrapped to H.R.H. the Duke of Gloucester. He approached the monument, removed the curtain, and when the statue was seen the joy in the hearts of Ethiopians was inestimable.[3]

Though paternal and colonial in his perceptions, Waugh's description conveys more accurately the flavor of the event.

> The square and half a mile of the avenue approaching it were lined with royal guards. A long pause preceded the Emperor's arrival. . . . Suddenly up that imposing avenue there appeared a slave, trotting unconcernedly with a gilt chair on his head. At last the Emperor came; first a troop of lancers, then the crimson car and silk umbrella. He took up his place in the centre of the court under a blue canopy. Then up the avenue came . . . the Marine band. The Emperor advanced, read his speech, and pulled the cord. The Emperor paused, listened attentively to the music, then smiled his approval . . . before driving away.[4]

Clearly the European press and the diplomats looked upon the coronation as playacting. Had it not been a serious display of Ethiopian pomp and circumstance, these European observers may have been excused, but recording these events with all the irony of caricature was gross in the extreme. Of course Haile Selassie's description was so serious and so stilted that it conveyed nothing at all of the circumstances surrounding the unveiling. What is clear is that Europeans saw this quite differently than the Ethiopians who were present. The various *rases* and priests saw a political or religious event of major proportion, while Europeans observed a ludicrous display, poorly carried off, of Ethiopians trying to be European. One thing is certain however, and here the European perception is absolutely correct. Ethiopians saw very little of the actual events unless they were members of the emperor's retinue. Throughout the reign of Haile Selassie this was a normal occurrence, as peasants and townspeople were always kept furthest away from the emperor. Another observer, an American, saw the unveiling and its concurrent discrimination of Ethiopians this way:

> Being foreigners, we always got the best places everywhere. The humble Abyssinians stood off at a distance, a considerable distance, and saw what they could. Yet some of these tribesmen had walked hundreds of miles to reach Addis, coming from provinces so remote that they had been marching for weeks to get here on time.[5]

Certainly, the emperor's statement that joy was seen in the hearts of all Ethiopians upon the unveiling of the statue was ludicrous, as few Ethiopians were present to see it.

The evening prior to the coronation there was a religious service at the Cathedral of St. George. The priests and deacons prayed and intoned through the night in the presence of the severe-appearing *Ras* Tafari and his wife, Woizero Menen. The priests "danced, chanted, beat their drums, and clapped their hands continuously. The costumes were brilliant and magnificent. Amidst the glitter of coronets, jewelled swords and gold braid, the traditional lion manes lent a truly African touch to the splendour."[6] Beating prayer sticks onto the ground in accord with the music, all the priests wore the traditional Ethiopian crosses hanging from their neck. Clouds of incense rose to the upper heights of the cathedral while the music and chanting drifted outside to the crowds which swelled ever larger as morning came. The soon-to-be-crowned emperor remained at the service throughout the night.

By 8 A.M. the dignitaries entered the church. For the ceremony the church had been enlarged by a very large tent. The emperor and empress were seated on golden thrones under a red velvet canopy held up by four posts made of gold. Ethiopian dignitaries sat on the right and the diplomatic corps on the left. "It was significant that no Abyssinian of humble rank could enter. . . . Only foreigners were allowed" to observe the coronation as guests.[7] Throughout the morning the assembled crowd participated in a high mass. Then the emperor, almost buried amidst gold, silver and red velvet, donned the robes of state and received the insignia of his office, orb, spurs, spear, and lances. At noon the crown, studded with rubies and emeralds, was placed on Tafari's head by the archbishop. Within a few minutes the archbishop placed another crown upon Tafari's wife, Woizero Menen, and slipped a diamond ring on her finger. Then the mass continued for a half hour. The emperor and empress, proceeding under the gold and red canopy, crossed to the stand and the emperor read his first proclamation as Haile Selassie I.

For the next few days the city was alive with celebration. Haile Selassie went among the populace distributing money while the people bowed and then lay prone as the emperor neared. Banquets, to which the emperor came, were held by various delegations, Ethiopian and foreign. As always, Haile Selassie remained aloof and distant. With a slight smile transfixed on his face he would arrive at a dinner, would be seated at the center of a top table, and throughout would sit stiffly, almost unmoving. A few words now and then to dignitaries seated next to him would force him to move slightly. The emperor then, and henceforth, was always keenly aware of his demeanor. Though polite, and often gracious, he usually gave the impression of being carved in rock.

At an audience once attended by the author in 1967, Haile Selassie was impressive, standing in the center of the room. All foreign guests bowed slightly, a bow he returned ever so subtly. Ethiopians moved to him, bent down to kiss his feet, and then prostrated themselves. He met each person with a fishlike handshake but with eyes that penetrated deep inside one. Dressed impeccably in a tailored European suit, he greeted each person individually, standing stiffly and appearing reserved. He was aware of his public appearance every second of the time. He was a monarch and each person there was made to feel it. His face was cragged and gave one the impression that years of history were bluntly written on it. Steeled and reserved and believing himself to be a giant of history, he made one forget that in fact he was a small man of slight build. Though he was younger in 1930, written accounts of meetings at that time with Haile Selassie portray the same concern with image and status. Distance must be kept. Christopher Clapham's recent description of him is keen.

> He is a very little great man, dapper and relaxed, his bearing upright, his handshake limp and his skin rather darker than most photographs would lead one to suppose; only his face suggests that force of personality which has infused Ethiopia for over fifty years. The short neat beard and the sharp downward droop of the moustache . . . still stamp his unmistakable features. His eyes are extraordinary; they stand out with a penetrating intensity which sometimes gives the impression that they are living an existence of their own, and looking at them, one can understand the feelings of those ministers who are said to tremble before him as a mouse before a cat.[8]

The ceremony attached to the coronation had both historical and political purpose. Historical in that the coronation provided a link with the past, a link with the imperial origins of the empire. Article Three, Chapter One of the 1931 constitution reinforces this point.

> The law determines that the imperial dignity shall remain perpetually attached to the line of his majesty Haile Selassie I, descendant of King Sahle Selassie, whose line descends without interruption from the dynasty of Menelik I, son of King Solomon of Jerusalem and of the Queen of Ethiopia, known as the Queen of Sheba.[9]

Thus tradition was institutionalized in the 1931 constitution, the first such document Ethiopia ever had.

Politically the ceremony was of vast importance to Haile Selassie. One major reason for inviting many foreign dignitaries was to convey through them to their governments that Ethiopia was entering a modern age. What the foreign reporters sneered at was precisely the point that the new emperor was making. The ceremony was awkward because Ethiopians were acting European. It was an attempt to clarify to observers that the emperor was trying to rid the country of traditional mores that might inhibit the new link that Haile Selassie was trying to create between Ethiopia and a much respected Europe. The occasion was therefore full of political symbolism.

On another level the emperor was impressing upon his own

populace that he meant to play a strong role in Ethiopia. He
would be a ruler of strong mind and one who was concerned
with continuing the modernizing policies of his father and of
emperors Theodore II and Menelik II. There was a European
flavor to the coronation but that was no accident. That was
policy, albeit symbolic, and it was a message that Haile Selassie subtly conveyed to his own people. Thus the coronation,
an event in itself, was also laden with a symbolism that looked
toward a new modern era.

There were also internal political dynamics associated with
the coronation. The new emperor made it clear at the time of
the coronation that he was unwilling to accept independent
power blocs that might be threatening to his own authority.
He would never, never again be second fiddle to anyone. The
title of king, which was held by Haile Selassie from 1928 to
1930, was not ever again granted to any noble. It was done
away with in conformity with the coming policy of personal
and political centralization, "thereby probably disappointing
certain expectations at the time of [the] coronation."[10]

The coronation ceremonies ended with entertainment that
was purely traditional Ethiopian and not pseudoEuropean. It
occurred on a plain just outside Addis Ababa. Thousands of
warriors passed before a reviewing stand, in costume. They
were "all dressed in white *chammas*, with lion skins, spears,
shields of rhinoceros hide, and war drums. In loose formation
. . . chiefs rode by, followed by their men. They swarmed
over the plain like ants, thousands of them, on and on, thump-
ing upon their war drums."[11]

So the massive celebrations came to an end, and a new era
for Ethiopians had begun. Haile Selassie, crowned emperor,
was the authoritative and sole ruler of Ethiopia, at least in
name. It would be years before he ruled in fact. But the
coronation was the signal that a new period had begun, one
that would bring Ethiopia more in line with twentieth-century
Europe. In addition Ethiopian notables were clearly shown
that the new emperor would attempt to place all power in his
own hands and would not permit countervailing authority to
limit his political prerogatives. Europeans were being shown
that relations between Ethiopia and their countries would be
altered. Ethiopia would attempt to Europeanize certain as-

pects of its political life so that the country would gain greater international legitimacy. This theoretically would create the conditions whereby Ethiopia could request aid from Europe to help in the political and military development of the country.

Haile Selassie was now in the position to rule and to start afresh in bringing a political program to Ethiopia that would reduce the power of the traditional *rases* and nobles. He had in mind changes that he would introduce throughout the period of his reign. How successful he would be in carrying out his program would be seen in the future. For now, however, Haile Selassie was freer than ever before to rule without the political inhibitions that had straddled him in the past. His reign began amidst great regalia and world attention. *Time* magazine devoted a large portion of a November 1930 issue to the coronation, while magazines and newspapers from around the globe covered the event. It was a public-relations coup laced with political overtones. Without question it was an event of importance for Haile Selassie, for Ethiopians, and for the world. Haile Selassie, the newly crowned emperor, would make his mark on history and would have an impact upon Ethiopia that few emperors of that ancient land had. He was now prepared to embark on a journey that would enable him to obtain a measure of power and control without precedent in Ethiopia. It was what he always wanted, what he desperately needed, and what he would, in the long run, get. He would, if he could help it, let nothing stand in his way. Control was now his and he was unwilling to share it or part with it. Personal control was now joined with political control, and the former would always affect the latter. Smug and self-satisfied, he had reached the pinnacle and he intended to remain there. He had every reason to be pleased with himself, and he was.

6. The Personal Centralization of Power

Speed and efficiency were the code words for the new emperor. He moved with a vengeance to secure total power in his person. It was almost as if Haile Selassie felt there was little time to lose if his authority were to be extended throughout the empire, and if those still opposed to his rule were to be vanquished. He was now in complete charge, he was the new youthful and strong Menelik II, and he was going to prove it—quickly. Since the emperor had always before been at the mercy of others due to the death of his father, *Ras* Makonnen, in 1906 when Haile Selassie was merely fourteen, he now resolved to create a political structure that would give him the personal security and political power that would allow him to control his own life and the lives of his subjects. No longer would he have to deeply bury his anger and hostility towards those who had tried to prevent his accession to the throne. He now proceeded in earnest to make his power felt and he directed his efforts primarily at centralizing the authority of government under his control, destroying the power of his opponents, and totally dominating Ethiopia. The coronation had been more than symbolic; it had legitimized his authority once and for all, and he was now prepared to exert it. His profound ambition could now be played out. Motivated by a sense of personal insecurity and deep mistrust, a belief that he was in a political position destined for him, a love of power, and a desire to Europeanize and modernize Ethiopia, he initiated a revamping of the political process, and a purge of his political opponents. It clearly did not take the emperor long to feel the sense of personal power he now had and it took him as short a period of time to exert that power. Power was his and he meant to use it.

Until 1931, the power of the national government remained completely in the hands of the emperor, and the crown served as a symbol and guarantee of the unity of Ethiopia. In 1931, however, Haile Selassie promulgated the first Ethiopian constitution and although he certainly did not relinquish power by this step, he institutionalized it, and established a parliament that was to serve him in ruling Ethiopia. There were apparently two prime motives for the establishment of the constitution. The emperor had always been concerned with Ethiopia's image abroad and the proclamation establishing the constitution was an attempt to improve that image. Also, the constitution was used as a means of destroying the traditional power bases of many of the *rases* who ruled the provinces.

> It aimed thus to eliminate gradually the personal and arbitrary power of the nobles by tightening the legal reins on its exercise. As long as the Emperor retained complete control of the constitutional process of legitimation—and the Constitution was designed to ensure such control—there would be no legal justification for such power.[1]

With one fell swoop Haile Selassie moved to centralize his authority and at the same time destroy the powers of his opponents. In his autobiography Haile Selassie claims that he wanted to set up a constitutional process while he was regent but the "Great Nobles" opposed it and he did "not wish to upset [Empress Zauditu] and do things by force (insisting that I was Regent). . . ."[2] His power at that time was frustrated, and his fury had to be held in check. Now, without having to fear the reactions of others, he moved with lightning speed to set up the constitution.

The crux of the constitution lay in Article Six: "In the Ethiopian Empire supreme power rests in the hands of the Emperor."[3] Imperial succession was reserved to the line of Haile Selassie, while "the person of the Emperor is sacred, his dignity is inviolable and his power indisputable."[4] All power over central and local government, the legislature, the judiciary, and the military remained with the emperor.

The executive government was institutionalized in that Haile Selassie formalized the existence of cabinet ministers in the constitution. As a result the executive office was divided between the emperor and the ministers, although the latter were appointed by, and responsible to, Haile Selassie. An attempt was thus made to streamline and modernize the bureaucracy which the emperor had originally initiated while regent. Under no conditions were ministers to have any independent power, and to retain their positions, they had to constantly prove their fealty and obedience to the emperor.

Parliament consisted of a senate and chamber of deputies. The members of the senate, or upper house, were appointed by Haile Selassie while the members of the chamber of deputies were selected by the traditional nobility and local chiefs in concert with the emperor. The size of the chambers, the duration of their sessions, and the lengths of terms of service were not specified in the constitution. Parliament was functionally powerless as Article Thirty-Four specified that "no law may be put forth without . . . having obtained the confirmation of the Emperor." John Markakis notes that the members of parliament "were certainly not intended to participate in decision making, since the letter of the Constitution limited their initiative to communicating to the Emperor any original suggestions they might have."[5] The judiciary had no right to interpret the constitution and no national authority whatsoever.[6]

Haile Selassie now had an instrument by which he could begin to neutralize countervailing forces. A number of the old nobility were appointed to positions in the senate in an attempt to socialize them into the modern political culture Haile Selassie was creating. In addition, by forcing them to come to Addis Ababa, where parliament was located, the emperor could keep an eye on their activities. Parliament, of course, also served as a place for honorable retirement without a full loss of status for those nobles whose traditional authority had been destroyed by Haile Selassie but whom the latter did not wish to alienate totally. Rather than serving as an instrument of legislation, parliament became a political tool of punishment or reward for enemies and allies. It was a status symbol totally without power, but allies could be rewarded with a seat, adding to their authority, and opponents could be punished by being "promoted" to a seat in parliament after having been removed from the source and location of their original power in the provinces.

The cabinet served a similar role styled differently. In 1931, and again in 1955 when a new constitution was promulgated, Haile Selassie utilized the cabinet to promote younger officials who essentially acted as a balance to the old nobility. Totally supportive of Haile Selassie and owing their position to him, this new elite, given land and power as patronage, allied itself with the emperor as against the powerful but independent landlords. This was the beginning of Haile Selassie's lifelong policy of balancing different groups, liberal and conservative, young and old, allowing each to do political battle with the other and in the process preventing any group from obtaining too much authority. But in 1931 the primary purpose of this maneuver was the neutralization of the old guard elite.

The innovation of parliament was also Haile Selassie's way of trying to impress Europe and European statesmen. It was, of course, style rather than substance; but it pointed out the genius of Haile Selassie in that parliament served to buttress and expand the traditional authority of the monarchy while in and of itself parliament is a symbol of modernism. Thus, Haile Selassie extolled his parliament as an indication of a changing Ethiopia while he used it to serve purely traditional political and personal purposes.

Reform was a key feature of the new constitution. Despite the fact that it served in a traditional capacity, it also reflected the emperor's lifelong concern with reform and his desire to create a political structure in a legal-rational mold that could, at some time in the distant future, replace the feudal system. He was deeply committed to reform, and to centralizing the processes of government so that Ethiopian peasants could get a better deal than the feudal system offered them. But the emperor was just as committed to preserving the monarchy and to slow evolutionary change. Reforming the system while preserving the feudal nature of society turned out to be impossible and eventually led to his own overthrow.[7] Though Haile Selassie successfully limited the national power of traditional forces, beginning the process in 1931, he could not allow them to be fundamentally destroyed because the entire regime rested upon a feudal land structure that Haile Selassie knew full well kept him in power.

Early in his reign Haile Selassie cared mostly about enlarging his own power and control—the contradictions that were to lead to his overthrow were not evident to him; in fact one of his major political flaws was that he never became aware of these contradictions.

Europe was incorporated into the centralization process as the emperor's attraction and appeal to European leaders finally began to pay dividends. A military academy was opened at Holeta during this period and a military mission came from Sweden to train the conscripts. Predominately Shoan, the new army was trained to defend both the nation and the emperor. The core of a semi-private military trained by Belgian officers, known as the Imperial Bodyguard, a crack contingent, was henceforth designated as Haile Selassie's personal military force. A small number of Amhara youth were sent abroad to France for military training. In this way a state military was created whereby Ethiopia would have a standing military force, indeed a tiny one to begin with, that would stand in direct opposition to the personal militaries that many in the old guard had at their personal disposal. This new military force would stand guard over the emperor but would be, and indeed soon was, used to consistently confront and destroy Haile Selassie's opponents. To reinforce his new military power, planes flown by European mercenaries were incorporated into the national army. Promulgating a constitution to centralize his authority was not enough to secure his throne and Haile Selassie knew this full well. His authority had to be reinforced by a standing military obtaining its authority directly from his person.

He now proceeded to eliminate his opponents. *Ras* Hailu, a totally independent member of the old nobility, ruled Gojam virtually with an iron fist. Believing strongly that Haile Selassie was sitting where another ought to, he consistently tried to reduce Haile Selassie's authority with the aim of throwing him out of office. In 1932 he was implicated in a plot that involved the escape of the former emperor Lij Yasu. Supported by Italy, *Ras* Hailu felt strongly that Lij Yasu could be used by him to topple Haile Selassie who had not as yet strongly secured his

throne. With Lij Yasu on the throne, *Ras* Hailu with Italy's
support would be a dominant power in Ethiopia. Haile Selassie moved quickly, and before any large-scale support could
be mustered by *Ras* Hailu. Stripped of all his properties he
was thrown in jail, while his son, who was then in Gojam,
was made to swear total fealty to the emperor. Some twenty of
Ras Hailu's associates were executed. Although *Ras* Hailu was
soon released and Lij Yasu quickly recaptured (he died in
prison in late 1932), Haile Selassie had strengthened his position measurably while *Ras* Hailu's power was functionally
neutralized. Not until the Italian occupation of Ethiopia
would *Ras* Hailu again be a threat to Haile Selassie.

In the North, in Tigre, Haile Selassie used more diplomatic
measures to limit the authority of two rival pretenders to the
throne, both of whom were related to the former Emperor
Yohannes. The crown prince was married to *Ras* Seyoum's
daughter, while a daughter of the emperor, Zanabe Work, was
married to the Tigrean Haile Selassie Gugsa. "Haile Selassie
hoped to frustrate the emergence of a united and separatist
Tigre"[8] through intermarriage, and though he succeeded he
was never really able to fully control either Tigre or Gojam,
the population of which directed their primary political attachment to either the feudal landlords who were able to
promptly and terribly exert their authority over the peasants,
or to their own communal leadership. But, for the short run,
Haile Selassie did succeed in increasing his authority to the
detriment of those who held a somewhat legitimate claim to
the throne.

Non-military measures were also taken to centralize authority and to generate a new reference group whose allegiance
would be directed both to the emperor and to the nation. Some
150 students were sent abroad for education while elementary
and secondary schools were established in Addis Ababa. This
group of students would eventually form the core of a new
elite that Haile Selassie hoped to use to secure the reforms he
had in mind. In addition, the Bank of Ethiopia was founded in
1931, issuing, for the first time, Ethiopian currency. A criminal
code was set up, and the country was divided into sixty-two
administrative units to finally put an end to slavery. Printing
presses were established in the capital to provide for nation-

ally oriented newspapers and for the publication of national legislation. And a select group of European advisors were brought to Ethiopia to fill positions in various ministries.

There can be no question whatsoever that 1930–1935 were the most important years in the long reign of Haile Selassie. Although only a few paragraphs are normally devoted to analyzing this era in most books on Ethiopia, it is during this period of time that the emperor truly established his authority. Though he had a legitimate claim to the throne, being a descendant of the Shoan dynasty of Sahle Selassie, others did too and they made it perfectly clear that they were unhappy with the present course of events. The old nobility had always been the true leadership of Ethiopia, rarely under the control and authority of emperors, and in their own provincial areas they did what they wanted and were beholden to no one. They owned tremendous parcels of land, taxed their tenant farmers mercilessly, had their own private military forces, and were often dictatorial in exerting their authority. Although their power was never destroyed, their ability to always dictate to any emperor was severely curtailed by Haile Selassie. They retained their land and remained feudal landlords, the source of their power, and they remained important political figures, but after 1931 they were never able to successfully and directly challenge the authority of Haile Selassie. The landlords and Haile Selassie came to recognize their dependence upon one another and the emperor came to believe that with their national power constricted, their authority over land should not be tampered with. This was fundamental to their power and Haile Selassie felt that if threatened in this area, they would successfully challenge his regime. The period between the coronation and the Italian invasion of Ethiopia was, then, of primary importance, one in which Haile Selassie took control of the national government and made it perfectly clear that he would strike hard at those who opposed his rule. But he made it just as clear that he would not attack the core of the nobles' authority, their control over peasants and land, in any fundamental way if they supported his right to rule. He might try to reform the worst elements of feudalism but he would not destroy it. Thus the emperor violently stilled those who wanted him out of power and he accommodated himself to those members of the old nobility that were willing to leave him alone if he left them alone. Feudalism was maintained, as it was throughout his reign, but national authority was left in the hands of Haile Selassie. The emperor was therefore able to quell the power of those who were out to destroy him, and at the same time he unassailably exerted his authority. Had he not done this, he never would have remained on the throne.

His scheme was brilliant. By creating new and independent sources of power he circumvented the necessity of allying himself with his primary enemies within the traditional elite. The military, European advisors, and students would be used to challenge and confront his opponents and at the same time would permit him access to a group of specialists independent of the old nobility and beholden to him.

Creating national institutions such as parliament and a central bank produced the structures through which he could exert national authority, but also suggested alternative political models to which the population could turn in times of need and distress. This was seen as severely hampering the traditional forces.

Most important, however, is that it is in this era that Haile Selassie, through the legitimation of his rule, created the circumstances by which he attained absolute personal fulfillment.

He was now in control, more or less, of the political system but totally in control of himself. Obtaining the prize of the throne is what Haile Selassie had always wanted and finally he had it. He no longer had to worry over what Empress Zauditu or other, lesser Ethiopian figures thought. He could unleash his authority when and under what circumstances he thought most propitious. In effect, for the first time in his life he was totally free—no longer having to concern himself over whether his actions would please some superior or lead to his own demise. All the aggression he felt while living in the palace during Menelik's reign, and after his death when political intrigue ran rampant and he was constantly in fear of his life, was unleashed. What was said about Catherine de Medicis can also be said about Haile Selassie up to this time. "Throughout her life she lacked the power to act directly to fulfill her desires, but she . . . compensated for this void with her manipulative skills."[9]

Haile Selassie no longer had to compensate and the anxiety he felt prior to 1930 finally had an outlet. He went after his opponent *Ras* Hailu with singular passion, and just as quickly acted to neutralize the authority of *Ras* Seyoum and Haile Selassie Gugsa. During the Italian occupation all three were compromised again and because of their collaborative activity, *Ras* Hailu and *Ras* Seyoum were kept under constant surveillance after the liberation while Haile Selassie Gugsa remained in exile. Wasting no time in trying to destroy their authority, Haile Selassie must have felt particular satisfaction in going after them. For they represented more than political opponents. They were symbols of Haile Selassie's newly acquired freedom and control. They were images of all those who, throughout the past, had threatened the emperor, causing him tremendous stress, anxiety, and insecurity. As Haile Selassie himself stated in describing *Ras* Hailu's behavior since 1928, "from the beginning all his activities had been of a deceitful nature";[10] but until he felt secure in power Haile Selassie had to bide his time. No more. Now he could freely and speedily act. His anger could now be directed at particular people, and the speed of the emperor's actions signifies the tremendous aggression that demanded release. Thus his enemies provided the instrument so necessary to the emperor's emotional sanguinity. Normally Haile Selassie did not have his opponents killed, but the execution of twenty of *Ras* Hailu's comrades greatly supports the hypothesis that the degree of his emotional anger was of explosive dimensions. He went after his enemies with orgasmic force, the level of which was seen again in 1935–36 and in 1960 when once again he was not in total control of either himself or Ethiopia. But there is little doubt that the emperor's frenetic activity during the years 1931–1935 was in large part due to the anxiety so long held in check, itself caused by the total feeling of helplessness and powerlessness that came from being at the mercy of others. Now he was the fulcrum and ecstatic to be in that role.

Fulfilled and feeling a complete person for the first time, Haile Selassie could hereafter afford to be merciful and fatherly, an image he did much to foster. But whenever he felt he was losing control, all the images of helplessness returned and he acted despotic and completely totalitarian. When this happened, one had to know that he was acting out his fears and anxieties of the past. Now, however, he no longer had to repress his feelings and his emotions. That had caused him too much distress in the past. He was at this moment a new man, one who finally had the opportunity to release that negative emotional energy that had been held in check too long. About the monarchy in general, but about himself most particularly, the emperor stated his own perceptions about his feelings at this time.

> If any man were to oppose or to infringe the Emperor's authority, the people's interests, or the power of the law, then he would, by his own will, have become an outlaw, and no defence whatsoever could be found for him to save him from punishment.[11]

Haile Selassie was now a happy and complete man indeed. But it had taken almost forty years of his life to attain this fulfillment, and with such a long period of repressing his feelings and emotions one could predict that whenever something happened that brought those hateful feelings back, he would aggressively lash out.

By 1935 Haile Selassie had broken away from his inner turmoil, though it would always be there in his subconscious to haunt him. In that year, however, events were occurring that would rob the emperor of his tranquility and temporarily strip him of his political power. Italy, which had been acting aggressively toward Ethiopia since 1925 when it unsuccessfully attempted to obtain a sphere of influence, invaded Ethiopia, and Haile Selassie's domestic policies had to be set aside. For he was now confronted with the gravest threat to his personal authority and well-being.

7. Denouncing Appeasement: The Conscience of Humanity

Italy's October 1935 invasion of Ethiopia had the most profound impact upon the Western world. The central figures of the disaster that was then unfolding before the eyes of the world were Haile Selassie and Benito Mussolini, the fascist ruler of Italy. But the centrality of their position was misleading. Adolf Hitler, in Germany, along with the leaders of France, England, and the United States were primary figures in that their positions relative to the Ethiopian crisis led almost directly to the havoc of the Spanish civil war, and then to World War II. Ethiopia was the first arena in the battle against fascist imperialism, and in this respect the actions of France and Great Britain were being closely observed by Hitler, who had his own imperial plans for Europe. While the Ethiopian war sent shock waves throughout the world, the implications of Italy's victory over an isolated Ethiopia were terrible. The refusal by the League of Nations to come collectively to the aid of Ethiopia and to adopt effective sanctions against Italy meant finally that the political preconditions to accepting war as the contemporary instrument for the annexation of national territory were established. At the time it appears that only four world statesmen then in positions of power were aware of the tremendous implications of the League's military impotence: Haile Selassie, British Foreign Secretary and Minister for League of Nations Affairs Anthony Eden, Adolf Hitler, and Benito Mussolini. Eden, during the Ninety-first Session of the League Council, meeting in Extraordinary Session April 20, 1936, maintained that "the seriousness of the consequences for

the League of the events of the last seven months can scarcely
be exaggerated."[1]

> The confidence which members of the League of Nations will feel
> justified in placing in this organization in the future must, in large
> measure, be influenced by its success or failure in the present in-
> stance. . . . There is in the principle of collectivity the one hope of
> lasting peace, for only by the strong endeavour of nations sincerely
> joined can the rule of law be substituted for the rule of force.[2]

Haile Selassie interpreted the position of the League as
broadly.

> I submit that the problem . . . is not merely a question of Italian
> aggression. It is collective security: it is the very existence of the
> League of Nations. It is the confidence that each state is to place in
> international treaties. It is the value of promises made to small states
> that their integrity and their independence shall be respected and
> ensured. It is the principle of the equality of states on the one hand,
> or otherwise the obligation laid upon small powers to accept the
> bonds of vassalship. In a word it is international morality that is at
> stake. . . . Placed by the aggressor face to face with the accomplished
> fact, are states going to set up the terrible precedent of bowing before
> force?[3]

The war and its surrounding events had three major consequences. Ethiopia was the first battleground of fascism and it
set the pattern for the expansion of fascist philosophy. In
March 1936 the German military marched into and occupied
the Rhineland, demilitarized by international treaty, and four
months later in July, the Spanish civil war erupted into which
Germany, Italy, and the Soviet Union sent aid and through
which Germany tested and honed its military machine. "With
the Italo-Ethiopian War, dictatorial aggression moved closer to
Europe, testing her powers and finding them devoid of decision and direction. Only if seen as part of this increasingly
tense and desperate drama does the struggle between the
Lion of Judah and Il Duce take on its full meaning."[4] By 1939,
when World War II began, Hitler had succeeded in taking
Austria and Czechoslovakia, while the Italians had completed
their invasion of Albania. Great Britain, France, and the
United States did nothing. The pattern of the takeover in
Ethiopia was adopted by superpowers and was utilized again
and again. Invasion by Germany or Italy was met with appeasement by Great Britain and France, and neutrality by the
United States. Ethiopia thus served as a testing place, an

experiment in the realm of military and international diplomacy, in much the same way as Spain served as a war zone through which Germany perfected its tactic of blitzkrieg or lightning war.

The failure of the League of Nations to invoke meaningful collective security against Italy caused the de facto destruction of that international organization. Caught up in the politics of the superstates, it remained powerless in the face of aggression until its final demise. Haile Selassie was prophetic in his analysis of the League should it fail to act in support of Ethiopia. The League was predicated on the principle of collective security and when the League abandoned this principle in Ethiopia, it destroyed faith in its future and set the precedent for further acts of appeasement toward the aggressor states of the era—Germany, Italy, Japan, and Russia.

Lastly, the attack by Italy set the stage for a minor political figure to thunder a historical and perceptive warning to the League that projected Haile Selassie to the world as an international statesman. For he spoke out at a time when others refused to and he attacked fascism when others feared to. With nothing further to lose, he said what was evident.

Anthony Eden, in his memoir *Facing the Dictators*, discussed the lessons of Ethiopia.

> If, as Clemenceau tells us, politics is the art of the possible, Hitler's occupation of the Rhineland was an occasion when the British and French Governments should have attempted the impossible. Hitler should have been called to order, if need be forcibly, at his first breach of an accepted international engagement. But nobody was prepared to do it. *The growing tendency to find excuses had been fertilized by the Abyssinian failure.*[5]

When Mussolini announced his decision to attack Ethiopia on October 2, 1935, few could have predicted the tumultuous events of the following decade that this incursion would set in motion.

The roots of the Italo-Ethiopian war of 1935 are found in the year 1896 when one of the most memorable battles in Ethiopian history occurred, the Battle of Adowa. In March of that year an Ethiopian army of some seventy thousand under the command of Emperor Menelik II thoroughly and soundly defeated an Italian invasion force made up of some seventeen thousand troops attempting to impose colonial rule upon

Ethiopia. Twelve thousand Italian soldiers were killed. The event was profound since it was the first time in the ugly era of European colonialism that an imperial force was stymied in its attempt to colonize an African state.

The immediate pretext for Italy's 1935 invasion was a relatively unimportant Ethiopian–Italian clash over a water hole. The incident had taken place ten months earlier, in December 1934, in Walwal, an Ogaden watering place on the Italian Somaliland–Ethiopian border to which Somali nomads brought their livestock. Italian troops and planes, with little difficulty, routed an Ethiopian unit and killed more than one hundred Ethiopian soldiers. Although the incident was little different from similar clashes, Italy and the Italian press refused to let the matter drop, and it became clear that Mussolini had decided to use the clash as a casus belli.

But it was Adowa and not Walwal that Mussolini had in mind when he addressed his people the morning of the invasion.

> For many months the wheel of destiny, under the impulse of our calm determination, has been moving toward its goal; now its rhythm is faster and can no longer be stopped. Here is not just an army marching toward a military objective, but a whole people, 44 million souls, against whom the blackest of all injustices has been committed—that of denying them a place in the sun. When in 1915 Italy mixed her fate with that of the Allies—how much praise there was from them, how many promises! But after a common victory, which cost Italy 670,000 dead . . . at the peace table these same allies withheld from Italy all but a few crumbs of the rich colonial loot. . . . We have waited patiently for redress in Ethiopia for forty years. Now—enough![6]

Ivone Kirkpatrick analyzes the motives of Mussolini more broadly, but supports the Adowa rationale.

> Italy needed both room for her expanding population and a source for raw materials which could be paid for in her own currency. There was the burning desire to erase the shame of Adowa. During the early months of 1935 a visitor was almost certain to find on the desk [of] Mussolini some book or other which referred to that battle or to the campaign. There was the ambition to raise Italy to the ambition of a Great Power; and a symbol of that status was an overseas empire. There was jealousy of . . . Hitler, who would shortly be able to deploy his newly found strength. Obsession with the glories of the former Roman Empire impelled him to renew them under the standards of fascism. He may have been attracted by the prospect of diverting public attention away from the internal economic difficulties . . . and towards external adventure. . . .[7]

"More substantial," says Denis Mack Smith, "was the matter

of prestige, because Mussolini urgently needed to reinforce in Italians the belief that fascism stood for something big, important, and successful."[8] With the invasion the machinery of the League of Nations was set in motion, Ethiopia had to militarily counter the attack, and Haile Selassie took on the mantle of international diplomat, playing, according to Arnold Toynbee, the "beau rôle"[9] in this international episode.

Italian troops crossed into Ethiopia from Italian Eritrea during the morning of October 3. In Addis Ababa local leaders had been called into assembly in the courtyard of the emperor's palace and the Grand Chamberlain read them the royal proclamation announcing mobilization. "The hour is grave. Arise, each of you. Take up arms and rush to the defense of your country. Repel the invader. May those who are unable because of weakness and infirmity to take an active part in this sacred quarrel, help Us with their prayers. All forward for your Emperor and for your country."[10]

The emperor and his military aides had obviously foreseen the impending attack, but their attempts to prepare for it had been belated, insufficient, and hampered by the League's refusal to come to the aid of Ethiopia. Modern arms were expensive and almost impossible to obtain because Britain and France were trying their utmost to placate Italy so as to prevent Mussolini from developing a political/military alliance with Hitler that would be threatening to the two European states. They therefore refused to sell arms to Ethiopia. The Ethiopian terrain, the ill-prepared nature of Ethiopia's regular and irregular forces, and the nature of their enemy—a well-equipped modern force of some 650,000 men, two million tons of materials, 400 war planes—dictated Ethiopia's dependence on guerrilla strategy.

Under the command of Marshal Emilio de Bono, who was later succeeded by Marshal Pietro Badoglio, the Italian troops eventually brought Ethiopia under Italian control. With the occupation of Addis Ababa on May 5, only three days after Haile Selassie had fled into exile, Mussolini, "from the balcony of the Palazzo Venezia, proclaimed to a delirious crowd the annexation of Abyssinia. . . . It was the moment of his life in which he savored his greatest triumph. He had avenged Adowa and wiped out the Italians' sense of inferiority."[11]

Ethiopia never stood a chance of defeating the Italian army.

As James Dugan and Laurence Lafore report, "the Ethiopian army was in large part tribal, in lesser part feudal, and in very small part modern. The Ethiopians won no single battle in the war."[12] Though *Ras* Desta and *Ras* Imru fought valiantly against the Italians, others, including *Ras* Hailu of Gojam Province, cooperated with the occupiers. A group of resistance fighters known as the Patriots failed in their attempt to prevent Italy from obtaining secure control of Ethiopia. The Italians, in addition to using the most modern of weapons, resorted to the use of poison gas to quell opposition. The Ethiopians, despite irregular military activities, were no match whatsoever for the mechanized Italian army, and victory was swift if not complete. In the course of the war and occupation hundreds of educated Ethiopians were massacred by the Italians in retribution for the attempted assassination of Rudolpho Graziani, the Italian military commander.

But what of Haile Selassie? What was his role in the unfolding events that were occurring in Addis Ababa, Geneva, Rome, and London? How effective was he vis-à-vis the Ethiopian military and what options, other than exile, did he have? Should he have fled Ethiopia? What were the motivations that led him to make the decisions he made and to go to Geneva to plead his case before the League of Nations? It is within the context of the battle for Addis Ababa, and the League of Nations, that his position will be analyzed. There is much controversy surrounding his decision to leave Ethiopia but if one is to understand why that option was chosen one has to comprehend the forces that were at work on the man.

Haile Selassie was now used to being in control, comfortable with the levers of power, and particularly adept at successfully striking at his opponents and coming out on top. Born into an Amharic and palace society where obedience to imperial authority was the rule, the emperor expected 100 percent loyalty. "The primacy of the court over all other functions appears at periodic audiences at the palace, when all high government officials and nobles are expected to pay their respects no matter what business may be pending in their offices. The chief value embodied in the status group of the new nobility as a whole has been that of loyalty to the sovereign."[13] Further, within the context of this Shoan–Amhara culture "the good man is . . . one who defends the land of his fathers, seeing that it is not sold to outsiders or that foreigners do not come to take it."[14]

The period between October 1935, when the invasion began, and May 1936 when Haile Selassie fled Ethiopia, was certainly extraordinarily traumatic for the emperor both politically and personally. For the first time as emperor he had lost complete control over events, was not able to dictate to an opponent, and had to bear military defeats and Mussolini's verbal slurs. Although he must have been aware intellectually that the battle against Italy was fruitless, the emotional toll on him was high, for this was a personal situation that brought him back to the helplessness he faced prior to 1930, but was new and alien in his role as emperor in that to cope with it was nearly impossible. The culture he was deeply imbedded in, and the only politics he knew, defined imperial life as one of authority, control, and manipulation. At the present moment he was unable to function within that framework and thus was as a ship being buffeted by crashing waves. He was as out of control as he was when his father died, and he was once again at the mercy of Empress Taitu, Empress Zauditu, and Habte Giorgis—only this time they were called Mussolini.

His failure in coping with the invasion was culturally and personally agonizing for him. For it defined him not only as unsuccessful but "ungood" within the context of his own culture. Menelik II had bravely and stunningly defeated Italy in 1896, becoming in the process a national and anticolonial hero. Haile Selassie's inability to engage Italy in the manner of Menelik II was surely a disappointment, and is painfully recalled by the emperor as one explanation of why he decided to go into exile.

> Since Our army had turned back in disarray, it was clearly a useless matter for Us alone to carry on the work together with a few of Our men. The plan which We had conceived . . . had remained unfulfilled. Similarly, all the places which We had intended to be used for fighting had been occupied by the enemy who had got there first. . . . We certainly encountered things which were troublesome for Our convoy.[15]

In his mind, staying on to fight the Italians was a useless endeavor. But more important, with each battle lost and with more and more of his men being killed while fighting under his banner, his own status was declining as he was becoming politically sterile. Being useless and unable to govern was psychologically devastating, for not only did *he* know it but his people knew it. On the eve of his departure from Ethiopia his frustration exploded into rage.

> The emperor's changed appearance showed only too plainly the agonized state of his mind. George Steer who saw him at the time was shocked: "He was dressed in khaki as a general. His aspect froze my blood. Vigor had left his face, his body was crumpled up, his shoulders drooped."[16]
>
> On Thursday night, in a fury of rage, he tore down the silk curtains from the baldachin of his throne, and shouted: "Take what you please, sack, loot . . . pillage."[17]

His people seemed to take him at his word as his departure signaled the beginning of looting and violence. As one observer noted, "The streets [of Addis Ababa] were filled with smoke, the flames were running from shop to shop, cars . . . were burning."[18] Del Boca describes the scene as one of absolute chaos. "Shiftas fought one another for booty and the Shoans took advantage of the wild confusion to shoot down their enemies, the Gallas."[19]

Haile Selassie, in his autobiography, denies that he called for the looting and destruction of Addis prior to his departure.[20] But given his state of mind, his utter desperation, his fury, his inability to rule, and his complete lack of control, it is highly probable that he exploded as reported. Certainly the looting would have occurred in any case, and it is not my purpose to place responsibility upon him. What is important here is why Haile Selassie had to leave Ethiopia. One cause certainly was the psychological state he was in. His culture did not provide escape mechanisms for such total failure by an emperor, and to remain in Ethiopia under these conditions became emotionally impossible. He had to leave, to escape the vice of his failure and to run from the homeland that confronted him daily with his impotence.

Pressures were also placed upon him by his wife and by some members of the old traditional elite to save his life, flee Ethiopia, and personally carry Ethiopia's case to the League of Nations—as they saw it the only hope for salvaging the situation. Haile Selassie, said to have pondered this throughout the evening of May 1, finally decided that the next day he would take the train to Djibouti and then sail to Great Britain. But it is vital to keep in mind that the emperor was already predisposed to flee into exile to escape the torment of his personal tragedy, and to save his own life. The pressures from *Ras* Kassa, Woizero Menen, and the Imperial Council only reinforced his own predilection. The rage he flew into on the eve of his travels and the hopelessness so evident on his face were so totally out of character and so alien to his personality that they had to come from one totally desperate. The aloofness and stoicism had momentarily been replaced by a raging inner frustration and helplessness that demanded an outlet. It pointedly symbolized how out of control Haile Selassie really was.

The only way out of this was to run. So he fled, releasing himself from his torturous bondage. But he combined his personal escape with political and diplomatic policy. He would go to Geneva to plead Ethiopia's case before the League of Nations, demanding of it adequate collective security measures that would save Ethiopia from Italian control, and would secure for him, once again, the power and authority of his throne. The League could then serve in two capacities. It would militarily aid Ethiopia, and in so doing would restore to him the personal control so necessary to his emotional existence. Going to Geneva also promised to recreate for him a semblance of control, for he would be in the company of statesmen and world leaders who would offer him respect, and would listen carefully to him, allowing him to view himself with the dignity and status that had eluded him for the past eight months. He would, in effect, regain a measure of personal control. This would be reinforced by the historical precedent of being the first leader of a country to appear before the League of Nations, and by spelling out clearly and forthrightly the world situation as he saw it.

Thus Geneva had a double purpose. It would project him as a world statesman, and it would allow him to once again be in control of events rather than being buffeted by them. John Gunther claims that what Haile Selassie believed "in most, after Ethiopia [was] himself. . . . Nothing really interest[ed] him except the giant task of holding Ethiopia together."[21] With faith in himself crumbling, and with Ethiopia being destroyed and occupied by Italy, Haile Selassie went to Geneva and then into exile, where he remained until January 1941.

Picked up from Djibouti by the British warship *Enterprise*, the emperor and his party sailed to Haifa, the port of British Palestine, on May 3. "The emperor was said, by people who saw him then, to be tired and worn, a pathetic figure now, with no trace left of the epic hero."[22] Put up at the King David Hotel in Jerusalem, Haile Selassie was all but ignored by embarrassed British officials. On May 23, accompanied by his wife, his two sons Crown Prince Asfa Wossen and the Duke of Harar, his daughter Tsahay, and by *Ras* Kassa, the emperor set sail for his permanent place of exile in England. Reaching London in the beginning of June, he was hailed by the British public who mobbed him at Waterloo station as a conquering hero. He had already become a symbol to many. The outpouring of love was exactly what Haile Selassie needed to deal with his wounded pride at having failed at home, and he remembered this moment with tenderness and joy. "At the railway station in London the British public gave Us a great welcome, and We then departed for the accommodation which had been prepared for us. The people assembled there demonstrated to Us their participation in our grief, and We admired the tenderness and kindness of the British people."[23]

Haile Selassie's finest hour in history was to come soon. While in London he was informed that the League of Nations was set to meet at the end of June to discuss the raising of sanctions against Italy. The still feisty emperor decided to address the assembly. His faith in the League intact, he hoped that, dominated by the liberal European states he so admired and wished to impress, Great Britain and France, the League would come to his aid. Also the meeting offered him the opportunity to catapult himself back into the orderly world of diplomats where some control could be exerted by his person. Accompanied by *Ras* Kassa, Wolde Giorgis Wolde Yohannes, and other Ethiopian dignitaries, Haile Selassie arrived in Geneva, the site of the headquarters of the League, on June 26, 1936.

The League of Nations, of course, had become entangled in the Italo–Ethiopian war almost from the very beginning. In October 1935 it had voted 50 to 4 to condemn the Italian aggression, and later voted limited sanctions against Italy. On the insistence of Great Britain, then under the helm of Prime Minister Stanley Baldwin, the export ban deliberately omitted such war-making essentials as steel, iron, oil, and coal, which made the sanctions absolutely innocuous. Eden, in his position as Minister for League Affairs, pushed hard for adequate sanctions but he was overruled by his cabinet.

> The issue between Eden and London was a fundamental difference of opinion. . . . The Cabinet had no enthusiasm for collective action, for a cooperative effort might mean trouble. . . . His superiors were convinced that Eden was far too dynamic at Geneva and were fearful that his drive for sanctions was incurring the risk of war with Mussolini; in spite of Eden's arguments—that a great power that did not lead would lose its greatness, that Mussolini was bluffing and would back down when he realized the unity and resolution of the League, that France would stand by Britain in the League, provided [it] were assured of British intransigence.[24]

The sanctions, which were seen as meaningless in terms of discouraging aggression, were a matter of great debate in the British cabinet which, because of the fear of driving Italy into German arms, was attempting to get them rescinded. Eden opposed this move, but it was the issue of sanctions that the League was to debate during the session at which Haile Selassie was to speak. The British cabinet and French government, neither of which was permitting arms to be sold to Ethiopia, were by mid-1936 pushing hard for an end to sanctions against Italy despite the warnings and pleas of Eden. In May Eden "was involved in [serious] discussions on the future of sanctions,"[25] and by mid-June the Cabinet had agreed "that sanctions would have to be called off soon, the question was where and when."[26]

Ethiopia's fate was sealed before Haile Selassie spoke at Geneva. England and France had decided to lift sanctions in an effort to appease Mussolini. Nevertheless the speech would be given and its impact would soar over the battlefield and have "the most lasting effect of anything [Haile Selassie] had ever done or would ever do again."[27]

The atmosphere at Geneva was one of doom and crisis. It was known that England and France would push hard for the removal of sanctions, and Eden and other delegates knew as sure as they knew anything that this would be the death knell of the League of Nations and its core, collective security. "I went to Geneva," said Eden, "in a depressed state of mind, to witness the final stages . . . of the Abyssinian conflict."[28] "The Emperor attended the Assembly. His behavior was, as always, brave, calm, and dignified. In that great audience his was probably the only mind at rest. He had done all he could. . . ."[29]

Haile Selassie was less nervous than he was comfortable. For he was in the presence of peers, of diplomats who admired his staunchness and attended his person. No longer was he running for his life, or faced with personal pressures of military and political impotence. He was being lauded by members of an international assembly who understood fully the import of what was taking place that day. Haile Selassie was excited at the prospect of once again being at the center of attention, this time in the presence of European statesmen representing countries Haile Selassie was so taken by and held in great respect. Ever since he first learned about Europe through the education afforded him by his father, he had been impressed with its modernism, and he knew instantly when he traveled there that he could be the instrument by which this modernism could be brought to Ethiopia.

Into the tense forum Haile Selassie made his entry. He had silently come into the hall where the assembly met and he sat quietly in the fifth row awaiting his call to speak. "He made his way to the rostrum, a small frail, tired figure in a white tunic and black cape."[30] As Del Boca described it, "Haile Selassie, wearing an ample black cloak that accentuated his pale face, so alive with intelligence, stood before the microphone. There was a breathless hush, and the eyes of all present were fixed on the slight, diminutive figure whose dignity Italian caricaturists had failed to destroy, whose spirit the Italian war machine had failed to break."[31]

As he was about to speak, the gallery was startled by members of the Italian press. Yelling as loud as they could, they shouted obscenities at the emperor, praised Mussolini and sent the Assembly into pandemonium. Nothing like it had ever occurred before. The emperor waited impassively at the rostrum, unfearing, strangely at ease, gazing "in quiet contempt at the hysterical Fascist journalists."[32] In some strange way he felt in total control and thus contempt and not anger was the emotion he felt. Everyone was waiting to hear from *him*, he was on center stage, and the world was anxiously anticipating what *he* had to say. Yes, he was in control. The emperor described the turmoil this way:

> When We . . . stood by the lectern, the Italians who had come there for news reporting started to whistle continuously with the intention of obstructing Our speech and rendering it inaudible. At this moment the Rumanian delegate [Nicola Titulescu] remarked to the President of the Assembly [Paul van Zeeland]: "For the sake of justice, silence these beasts!" ["a la porte les sauvages!"]. The President of the Assembly, ordered the guards to expel the Italians by force; they then seized them and ejected them.[33]

The emperor then went on to give what can only be termed the speech of a lifetime. It riveted his audience to attention and confronted them as never before with the reality of their position. "I, Haile Selassie I," he began, "am here today to claim that justice which is due to my people. . . . There is no precedent for a head of state himself speaking in this Assembly. But there is also no precedent for a people being victim of such injustice, and being at present threatened by abandonment to its aggressor." After reviewing the military and diplomatic events of the past eight months, he came to the core of the issue. "The problem submitted to the Assembly today is . . . collective security: It is the very existence of the League of Nations. . . . God and history will remember your judgement."[34]

The League Assembly was listening to its funeral oration, for Haile Selassie warned it that should it continue to withhold support for Ethiopia, the Covenant of the League would be held worthless, and the League would become an international fossil. He called upon the League to enforce Article Ten of the Covenant, which states that "The Members of the League undertake to respect and preserve as against external aggression the territorial integrity and existing political independence of all members of the League." This "Guarantee Against Aggression" (as Article Ten was entitled) was the core of collective security and was reinforced by Article Sixteen: "Should any member of the League resort to war in disregard of its covenants under Articles Twelve, Thirteen, or Fifteen, it shall *ipso facto* be deemed to have committed an act of war against all other members of the League, which hereby undertake immediately to subject it to the severance of all trade or financial relations. . . ."

But the emperor's deeply moving and prophetic warning to those who were trying to bury the League of Nations met with no success. On July 15, pressured by Italy, France, and Great Britain, the League voted to lift its sanctions against Italy. The admiration that League members had for Haile Selassie could not be translated into collective security. For in reality, collectivity meant France and Great Britain opposing Italian aggression and neither state was prepared to override its national interests for the sake of international law or morality. Their national interests contradicted what collective security would have required them to do. The ideally perfect scheme as embodied in the League Covenant was buried under political reality. "The first great attempt," according to Inis L. Claude, Jr., "to create a collective security organization was for all practical purposes terminated."[35] And as Haile Selassie said in 1954, "The League of Nations failed and failed basically because of its inability to prevent aggression against my country."[36]

In this way Haile Selassie became the conscience of humanity in 1936. The fear of his own violent death at the hands of the Italians or of the certain humiliation they would have subjected him to as their prisoner, combined with a desire to once again be in personal control of events, pushed him into the forum of the League of Nations. Though he failed to rally the League to action, his stirring words offered the world a signpost toward the eventual opposition to the fascist aggressors, Italy and Germany. Winston Churchill, then a member of the British Parliament and no mean orator himself, blamed the Baldwin government for the whole mess, advancing the thesis that had it stood behind the emperor and Anthony Eden, the world would have progressed differently. "The fact that the nerve of the British Government was not equal to the occasion . . . played a part in leading to an infinitely more terrible war. Mussolini's bluff succeeded, and important spectator[s] drew farreaching conclusions from the fact."[37]

The London Times maintained that "for the little good it can do him now, Haile Selassie has and will hold a high place in history. His legend may not be without a growing force hereafter."[38] After his moment in history Haile Selassie repaired to Bath, England, remaining there in exile until his return to Ethiopia in January 1941 with British troops. Living poorly with the help of monies donated by pro-Ethiopian societies, Haile Selassie spent four years contemplating his return to Ethiopia. With much time to think and read, he was determined that the powerlessness that affected him during the Italian onslaught would never again occur. He would rule with an iron hand and would once again attain the fealty from his subjects that he deserved. These were times of brooding and depression, of contemplation and planning, of aloneness in exile. Short walks, periodic meetings with British officials and dictating his memoirs were pleasant interruptions in a powerless and empty life. Haile Selassie was now used to power and wanted it back, but he wanted it on his terms. He would get it in time. But he knew that he was no longer just an Ethiopian monarch; he had transformed his image and was now considered a world leader, an international man without a country. He was a statesman and that thought kept him going during moments of gloom and self-doubt. For if the word *statesman* means anything it relates to the ability to foresee events and the ramifications of those events. In June 1936 Haile Selassie did just that. He was also able to portray these events in such stark and eloquent terms that his League of Nations speech itself became an event and an important part of history: the war and Haile Selassie's presentation before the League were seen as two vital parts of the same whole, both having their impact upon states, leaders, and peoples. The speech was his finest hour and no one single moment in Haile Selassie's life would ever come close to matching that moment. He had turned personal and political adversity into a historic pronouncement that made him a hero.

He thus regained, in his own mind, some of his lost ego, stature, and authority, the absence of which had caused in him such personal feelings of inferiority. The trip to Geneva had turned out exactly as he had hoped, at least on an emotional level. His ego intact once again he felt sure that he could return to Ethiopia without the guilt that had so haunted him from October 1935 to May 1936. He would once again be the "good" man, the effective emperor, comparable to Menelik II, and he would be able to command without feeling insecure or weak. No one would be able to say he fled Ethiopia in its time of adversity, for he had played, at Geneva, a pivotal role in molding world opinion. He was now emotionally whole. Never again if he could help it would he permit himself an explosion of rage, for henceforth power would be his and his alone—he hoped. If Geneva did not succeed in getting the League to isolate Italy it served the more important purpose of allowing Haile Selassie to reconstruct his identity and to rebuild his inner self. Geneva thus served for him a personal, rather than political purpose which was more or less what Haile Selassie had in mind. He emerged from Geneva an emotionally complete person once again, and he could not help but be pleased.

8. The Contradictions of Absolute Rule

The return of Haile Selassie to Ethiopia in January 1941, and his arrival in Addis Ababa four months later, marked the beginning of a twenty-year struggle to finally achieve full and absolute power over all his subjects. Throughout this period the emperor would find himself pressured by modern and traditional forces, each attempting to push him in different political directions. Unsure himself of which position he preferred, he gave a little to each group and in return demanded support from both. "Much of Haile Selassie's success has been due to his manner of balancing the different groups, listening to each and granting some of its aims, thus preserving a degree of consensus and preventing any group from openly challenging his regime."[1]

The duality of the cultural influences impressed upon Haile Selassie by his father, *Ras* Makonnen, would become fairly evident during this era. Haile Selassie's infatuation with things Western would lead him to join together with the United States in a political/military alliance of benefit to the emperor in his move to attain complete control of Ethiopia. The United States would supply the emperor with the weapons and aid so necessary to keep power and to expand it. At the same time he would begin the process of trying to limit further the influence and power of the landed nobility—both old and new—indicating that at this point Haile Selassie felt there was more to gain for him and for Ethiopia by leaning towards the modern elements of society as against those serving tradition. But he would notice, for perhaps the first time, just how powerful the landed elite were and often Haile Selassie would have to retreat from his political positions. Necessary to the successful attainment of power was the handling of the dual cultural realities that would act to dichotomize the emperor and eventually lead to his ouster.

From 1941 to 1959 Haile Selassie would succeed in retaining such personal control over Ethiopia that his ego would be as satiated as it would ever be. Though always fearful of losing control and always aware of the threats to his physical and emotional security represented by figures from his past, the emperor would see his anxiety reduced markedly because he attained a measure of control that he had never had before. His self-satisfaction was indicated in an interview granted to the *Voice of Ethiopia* in 1959. In response to a question, he stated that "Our strong determination has enabled Us to get over the obstacles presented by the [Italian] war and to patiently lead Our people to the comparatively high level in which they find themselves today."[2]

When Haile Selassie reentered Addis Ababa May 5, 1941, leading a joint British–Sudanese–Ethiopian army against the Italians who were now in retreat in Ethiopia from the Allied powers who had gone to war against Germany and Italy in 1939, he claimed that "today is a day on which Ethiopia is stretching her hands to God in joy and thankfulness."[3] He requested that all Ethiopians show mercy to the Italians and "do not return evil for evil, do not indulge in atrocities."[4] The emperor could afford to be generous. He was merciless only when directly confronted with a full loss of control, but on this Victory Day he was back in power, again the center of the Ethiopian universe, in full control of himself and his country. With British support Haile Selassie embarked upon the restoration of his authority and the reintroduction of programs that would serve to centralize his personal power as never before.

In accord with the Anglo–Ethiopian agreements of January 31, 1942, and December 19, 1944, Ethiopia was forced to accept British demands that all Ethiopian acts relating directly or indirectly to the war effort against the axis powers of Germany, Italy, and Japan receive Britain's approval. In effect, until 1951 Great Britain oversaw Ethiopian sovereignty. This temporary arrangement served Haile Selassie very well as it allowed him to concentrate on normalizing domestic matters while Great Britain policed Ethiopia, seeing to it that opposition to the emperor was kept in check. Great Britain, realizing the importance of Ethiopia to the Suez Canal and to Egypt, where Allied interests were formidable, was intent on keeping Ethiopia on the side of the Allies and therefore aided the emperor in securing his authority. It was an arrangement that Haile Selassie was very good at procuring for himself and in many ways it served as the model for the more important pact that would soon be arrived at with the United States—then in the process of becoming the most powerful industrial state in the world. While the British watched, Haile Selassie, under their protection, acted.

Control of the landed elite was first on the list of priorities established by the emperor. Although Haile Selassie remained unwilling to directly challenge this plutocracy, he was adamant that their ability to influence the position of the national government be stymied. In order for the restored government to act effectively, it needed a steady flow of funds, and through the establishment of a land tax system Haile Selassie hoped to be able to collect monies that would (1) allow him to rule efficaciously and (2) reduce the power of the landed nobility.

The first major economic reform attempted by Haile Selassie showed how rapidly the landlords and the provinces would act to preserve their vaulted position. Under Proclamation No. 8 of March 30, 1942, announced in the newly established *Negarit Gazeta,* the official government gazette, the emperor, without recourse to parliament, ordered a system of taxation that would, he hoped, help stabilize the government and his position in it. Accordingly, all land was to be divided into categories of fertile, semifertile, and poor, and a specific levy of E $15, E $10, and E $5 respectively for each *gasha* (40 hectares) of land was proclaimed. Land was to be measured and classified for the first time in history, and it was ordered that "every landowner shall be liable to pay tax at the rate specified."[5] Although this appeared simple enough, it could never be effected.

The first to rebel were the people of Gojam, Tigre, and Beghemdir. In these provinces the communal land tenure

structure was as old as time and derived from the principle
that land is divided among children, and among the children
rights are based on usage rather than ownership. According to
Mann and Lawrance "in Gojam, where land is held communally by members of an extended family, only the name of the
family founder, who may have died hundreds of years ago, is
entered [on the tax register], and there is no record at all of
present-day owners."[6] These three provinces, particularly
Gojam, fought off tax assessors, prohibiting them from
measuring land. Fearful of the disruption of the communal
land tenure system that would identify owners and then place
them at the mercy of the central government, Gojam, "which
was virtually independent of political control from the centers
of Amhara power,"[7] successfully battled the government over
this issue. In Proclamation No. 70 of September 11, 1944, the
three communal provinces were excluded from the standard of
taxation imposed by the earlier proclamation. At this time
Haile Selassie was not secure enough politically to throw his
country into a civil war over taxes and he beat a hasty retreat
when confronted with unified and wide-ranging opposition.

Landlords too bristled at the 1942 Proclamation and made
clear to Haile Selassie that they did not view the tax structure
as merely reformist but as an attack upon their base of power.
The landlords made it apparent that they had no quarrel with
Haile Selassie's right to rule Ethiopia, but when that right to
rule encroached on their land system, then they objected;
Haile Selassie understood, did not feel threatened personally,
and excused from payment via the 1944 taxes landholders of
rist-gult (a form of land tenure granted by emperors to those
members of the royal family who rendered him service), *siso-
gult* (a variation of *rist-gult*), and *samon* (land in which the
primary interest is vested in the Ethiopian Orthodox Church).[8]
With the Church and the landlords in fundamental opposition
to his policy, Haile Selassie wisely retreated. With the exception of the Church, however, all owners of land were now
required to pay to the government the 10 percent tithe traditionally collected by landlords from tenant farmers.

The 1944 Proclamation, therefore, left the farmers in the
communal provinces functionally free of land taxation since
ownership could not be verified, totally exempted the Church

from the payment of any land taxes, and required only that landowners whose land was not covered by traditional and ancient land tenure systems pay the land tax to the government. What the landlords did was to refuse to pay the tax and to either retain the tithe for themselves, in addition to privately taxing their tenant farmers via traditionally vested authority, or force the tenants to pay an additional tithe that went to the government, which was blatantly illegal but which the emperor had no control over. "It is clear from the land tax proclamation that the landowner is the person liable to pay . . . tax. It is quite clear that the intention of the legislation was that the burden of the taxation should fall not on the farmer, but on the landowner only. This . . . has not been implemented. In Ethiopia, this shifting of the tax burden . . . has been tolerated by the Government for many years."[9]

The conflicting strains of modernization and tradition came full circle in the years 1942–1944. Though intent on reducing traditional sources of power through modern means, Haile Selassie was just as aware that if he wanted to remain on the throne he would have to bow to the forces of tradition when they felt acutely threatened. A threat to them was in the final analysis a threat to him. Although the 1942 program was wide-ranging and universal, the 1944 policy was restrictive and particular. The emperor had gotten only a very little of what he truly desired but he was not unhappy as his retreat from policy allowed landlords to rightfully believe the emperor would not try to destroy them, and thus they were perfectly happy to leave him alone. Inadvertently the emperor had secured his position in 1944 because landlords no longer feared him. He would functionally do their bidding in terms of land policy, leaving the feudal land system intact. Thus they left him free to engage in policy-making that did not infringe upon their rights. The 1942/1944 tax burden "fell entirely on the shoulders of the peasant cultivator, where it [had] been since time immemorial, while the landholders not only escaped taxation but also continued to appropriate part of the taxes they collected for the state."[10] In 1951, after years of additional pressure by landlords, Haile Selassie reduced even further the land tax payable by those landlords not covered by traditional tenure exemptions.[11]

The major traditional elements within Ethiopia—the Church, the landlords, and the communal provinces—were each capable of causing Haile Selassie an extensive amount of political trouble that might have threatened his ability to maintain himself on the throne. Although a reformer, the emperor was extremely realistic and recognized that he and the traditional forces shared a common goal. Both wanted to preserve their own power and the sources of that power. Alone Haile Selassie could not stand up to traditional elements. There existed at this time no countervailing political force other than the military which was then extremely weak, having been all but decimated during the Italian invasion and occupation. The British would try to ensure that no manifest opposition to the emperor arose, but even they would not have been able to put down the massive disorder that would have exploded had the emperor pushed for his land tax or land reform program. Haile Selassie was not a fool and though he underestimated the effects on the nobility of his program for change, when they did become known to him, he removed the threat to traditional forces. In addition Haile Selassie was tied to these groups insofar as he was himself a primary representative of Shoan–Amhara culture. The landlords, the emperor, and the Church hierarchy were of the same class and all accepted the values inherent in upper-class existence. Haile Selassie, however, was caught up in a contradiction in that he also believed in modernization which in political terms meant reform of the worst excesses of feudalism. But he was beginning to learn that reform was anathema to the elite class and that they would not stand for it. Being the paramount representative of the ruling class whose overall values appealed to him and at the same time playing the role of reformer entailed a contradiction difficult to resolve. And the only way he could deal with it was to advance a policy and then retreat from it if there were too much opposition. Haile Selassie was not committed enough to modernization to push for the destruction of a culture he was so very much a part of. Had he been, he would not have lived a very long time for he would quickly have been toppled from power by the ruling feudal class. In essence, though he believed he was a reformer, his commitment to feudal society was too overwhelming to allow the reformer in him to succeed. His need to control and his instinct for survival were such that he would rather rule a politically stagnant Ethiopia than possibly be overthrown for attempting to do the brave and right thing. Haile Selassie was never aware of this contradiction or where it would eventually lead. For the time being he had to look elsewhere for funds to rule his empire and he had to begin the process of creating a countervailing group that could help him stand up to the landlords.

In a contradictory move that aimed at modernizing government fiscal practices, but which was oriented toward traditional forces, Haile Selassie issued a Personal and Business Tax Proclamation: Proclamation No. 60 of 1944. These first-ever income taxes were levied equally on all income levels, which in itself was a sop to the ruling elite, for as Gerhard Colm states, "the social-critical ideology . . . seeks to establish a tax system which . . . taxes the rich more heavily than the poor."[12] Since opposition to a progressive income tax was intense among the ruling class, this regressive tax was proclaimed and once again the poorest classes of Ethiopia were burdened beyond their means. The tax was based on a series of schedules that taxed income from employment, income from rents of lands and buildings, and income from business. Moreover, under Article 8[13] the Minister of Finance was empowered to exclude from payment certain unspecified categories of taxpayers, which, of course, meant that he could use his authority to aid those who wished to avoid having their income taxed. As usual, then, it was the poorest who were responsible for coming up with the money that would allow Ethiopia to function fiscally.

Although the largest amount of income from direct taxes came from the income tax, the specific figures give remarkable insight into who paid and who didn't and how ineffective government really was in this matter. In fiscal year 1965/66 with an estimated population at the time of some 27 million, with the real wealth of the state being locked up in agriculture, government revenue by source included: Income Tax—$E33.8 million, Land Tax—$E5.5 million, Tithe—$E10.5 million, Alcohol Tax—$E17.0 million.[14] One should note that whereas land tax in fiscal year 1965/66 brought in only 1.5 per

cent of ordinary governmental revenue, the alcohol tax, which
had been put into force in April 1965 and was directed almost
solely at the working class, was 5 percent of the *total* ordinary
revenue. In this case, figures are an accurate indication of
where the tax burden fell and how completely ineffective the
government was in its ability to collect land and income taxes
from the rich. Most landowners flatly refused to pay any
taxes[15] and according to the Ministry of Finance, if all available land were properly taxed at the existing rates, instead of
$E5.5 million, land taxes would have amounted to a minimum
of $E37 million and a maximum of $E131,600,000.[16]

Once again Haile Selassie had to content himself with obtaining an absolute minimum in revenues because of the clout
wielded by the landed elite. The ordinary workers in the cities
and the tenant farmers in the interior were mercilessly taxed,
and were thus forced to support the ruling class of Ethiopia.
The most important methods of holding the loyalty of the
elites were through the distribution of land, the allowance of
traditional and modern tax shelters, and a regressive income
tax. Acting individually but sharing values with the emperor,
the ruling class nullified the measures that Haile Selassie felt
compelled to enact. This was not an attempt to undermine his
imperial position but to preserve intact the sources of its own
regional power and authority. In the face of such opposition,
and not feeling that his own position was threatened, Haile
Selassie made no move to rigidly enforce the provisions of the
income tax regulations. They remained on the books and were
generally directed at the working class while the ruling class
retained its power free of all but the most minor government
regulations.

A customs office was set up in 1943 and export duties that
were generally enforced were announced, while in 1947 Proclamation No. 94 established an education tax amounting to 30
percent of the sum of the land tax and tithe payable on land.
The latter tax was shifted by landlords onto tenant farmers. It
was evident that, until Ethiopia and its ruling group could be
fully integrated within the emperor's authority, most taxes
would continue to be paid by the poorest classes. In order
therefore to strengthen his own authority and control, Haile
Selassie embarked on an ambitious program that would bring

about reform of the institutions of government. As I have stated elsewhere, "[spreading] the authority of the government and then creating a multiplicity of [central and regional] political institutions to carry out the government's demands, the Emperor . . . tried to limit the power of traditional forces in Ethiopia by decentralizing the central political authority."[17]

Concurrent with the establishment of tax laws, Haile Selassie reorganized the government in an effort to escape the contradictions that continued to make him helpless in the face of the landed nobility. He was intent on reforming the system and thereby generating control over his opposition. Exerting control was fundamental to his character and had been since the anxiety of his teenage years. Though not a direct threat, the landlords were questioning his authority and control, creating within the emperor a moderate degree of anxiety. Although of the class they represented, he was still insistent on exerting control over them, which indicated just how powerful were the influences of his insecure youth.

One of Haile Selassie's major programs was to institutionalize local government and place it in the hands of the central government in Addis Ababa. By creating a new set of regional elites, Haile Selassie hoped to neutralize to some degree the traditional landed elite. Decree No. 1 of 1942 set up the political subdivisions of the country and established corresponding political roles. Each of the provinces[18] was placed under the responsibility of one governor-general who was appointed by the emperor. A number of lesser officials also appointed by Haile Selassie were to aid the governor-general in seeing to it that taxes were collected and that government regulations were carried out. Each province was subdivided into subprovinces *(awurajas),* which were subdivided into districts *(waredas),* and subdistricts *(mektilwaredas).* Each had a governor appointed by the emperor to oversee the local area under his authority. A local militia was also established but the rules regulating its use were strict to prevent governors-general from utilizing this force for personal reasons or against the emperor.

> In the event of serious disturbance in the province beyond the powers of the police to cope with, the governor general is authorized to call upon the military forces in his province for assistance. He must

first of all consult with a commission consisting of the senior officials
of the various ministries who may be present, the commanding
officer, and five chief elders, and must also notify the [emperor] of his
intention . . . and shall await his instructions.[19]

All power was theoretically in the hands of Haile Selassie
but according to Perham, "the emperor found it necessary to
appoint older men of standing" as governors, "and to give
scope and practical expression to the desire for reforms of the
younger men . . . the emperor appointed some of these as
directors" who were aides to the governors.[20] In 1962 when
Haile Selassie wanted to give real political clout to new provincial elites in the provinces, both parliament and landlords
raised such havoc that Haile Selassie had to back down—and
fast.[21]

Decentralization proved interesting. A modern institutional
technique set up to limit traditional powers, it was utilized by
these elites to serve their own interests. They were the ones
appointed to the positions of governor and governor-general
and thus they were placed in political structures through
which they could enlarge their power and their landholdings.
The emperor had originated the structure but landlords took it
over. Now peasants were even more at the mercy of the ruling
class as regional political positions were filled by the same
landlords they worked for. The feudal system legitimized itself in modern political structures that reinforced traditional
rules of political behavior, and as such feudalism embedded
itself in legal structures and statutes. The traditional elites
would allow the emperor to appear as a reformer and even to
create structures that implied reform of feudalism but they
would not permit its effective operation. Once again Haile
Selassie failed to implant structures of reform effectively, and
as usual it was the peasant and tenant farmer who lost most in
this reform/tradition game being played by the ruling class. No
matter what he did, Haile Selassie could not buck the feudal
system, nor did he really wish to since it would have meant his
own demise. So he remained satisfied to appear as a reformer
while functionally upholding the rights of the traditional elite.
Not until 1967 would the emperor again seriously attempt to
control feudalism. An unwritten and unstated concord was
reached between the emperor and the ruling class in which

the former would not encroach upon the landlords and they would not intrude upon his rule in areas of national interest. He made it clear that any attempt to undermine his imperial position would be dealt with firmly.

For the time being the contradiction of the duality of cultures was resolved. Haile Selassie's mantle of reform of feudalism would be put aside while he tentatively accepted the imperial guardianship of the overlords of feudalism. He would direct his concentration into other areas while making only minor inroads into reforming feudalism. Ironically his position was strengthened through the weakening of his authority. This was another contradiction that would return later to haunt him. To compensate for his regional weakness, Haile Selassie tightened up the national government. The office of prime minister was created,[22] the powers of other ministers were specified and, together, this council of ministers was responsible to and appointed by the emperor. With the number of ministries enlarged to eleven, Haile Selassie brought some younger personnel into office so as to weaken the old elite's role in national affairs. A new national court system was also constructed and all judges were chosen by Haile Selassie. In 1955, in an attempt to "provide a new basis of legitimacy designed to attract the loyalty of the modernizing sector"[23] a new constitution was proclaimed by Haile Selassie.[24] New institutions were established in the executive office, and the power of parliament was increased.

The executive office, under the new constitution, included a council of ministers, the crown council, and, of course, the emperor. The council of ministers, consisting of a prime minister and all the cabinet ministers, was an advisory body to the emperor. As spokesman of the emperor in parliament, the prime minister, together with cabinet ministers, served without any fixed term of office and were appointed to their respective positions by the emperor and could be removed by him.[25] All draft bills were to go to the council for study. The council would then present its recommendation to the emperor who in turn would present the bill to the crown council. It consisted of the archbishop of the Ethiopian Orthodox Church, the president of the senate, and other dignitaries appointed by the emperor. "Decisions made in Council and approved by the

Emperor shall be communicated by the Prime Minister to Parliament in the form of proposals for legislation."[26] A private cabinet never formally established but wielding great influence upon the emperor also came into existence at this time.

Under this newly established structure, Haile Selassie tried to please both traditional and modern groups and also attempted to pit them against one another. The council of ministers was made up of some of the emperor's closest allies some of whom supported his attempts at bringing change. Through the establishment of the University College of Addis Ababa in 1951, which became known as Haile Selassie I University, the emperor saw to it that younger men with reformist leanings would be trained to fill lower-ranking positions in the cabinet and would then serve to aid the emperor in carrying out reform programs. While the cabinet represented some degree of reform, the crown council and the private cabinet represented the most traditional and archaic elements of Ethiopia. Fearful of and resistant to change, the men who filled positions in these two structures were of the traditional elite and until 1967 succeeded in neutralizing the power of the cabinet and parliament.

The 1955 Constitution expanded the powers of parliament by requiring that proposed legislation be submitted to it, and in order to become law, such legislation had to receive the approval of both the senate and the chamber of deputies. Senators continued to be appointed by the emperor but members of the chamber of deputies were to be elected by universal suffrage. Through the use of appointment and property qualifications necessary to sit in both houses, the emperor could control representatives of the old elite, but at the same time traditional forces through their control of the provinces could ensure overwhelming representation in parliament.

Since parliament remained a rubber stamp until 1967, the new constitution really served to institutionalize within the national government the struggle between modernization and traditionalism. But the cards were stacked heavily in favor of tradition, for Haile Selassie was fearful of allowing modern forces to get out of hand and threaten the landlords who would then turn their anger directly upon him. Although the emperor produced a modern constitutional structure, once again it was taken over by traditional forces, but this time with the emperor's approval because after 1942 he had seen that the maintenance of his power rested with the landlords. The new constitution gave the appearance of change but indeed changed very little. Haile Selassie had chosen to side with the landlords but to appear to support the forces of modernization.

The first official prime minister under the new constitution was Aklilu Habte Wold, a man who precisely represented the forces impinging upon Haile Selassie. Young and educated in France, he was a product of modern forces, but as a Shoan–Amhara, he was never inclined to challenge the major traditional figures that he had to work with. He was competent "without trying to upset the balance of power within the government"[27] that was heavily tilted towards tradition.

Much has been written from the perspective of political science regarding Haile Selassie's efforts to reform the political process in Ethiopia.[28] The varying opinions are that Haile Selassie was trying to legitimize his personal rule by the establishment of modern institutions, that he was attempting to limit the influence of traditional forces, or that he truly represented a feudal class but organized modern political structures to impress the West. Another hypothesis is that the dual cultures that Haile Selassie had been trained in as a youth imposed upon him the belief that he was a man of two worlds with one foot in each and that he could accommodate both Western and Shoan–Amhara tradition through his rule. To state it a bit differently, he was initially confused as to which culture he really believed in and was thus unsure of which group he should throw his support to. His father, *Ras* Makonnen, had trained him well and as a result Haile Selassie could be conceived as being a man without a dominant culture that he felt at ease with. The years from 1942 to 1955 represented a period of time through which Haile Selassie attempted to work this out in his own mind. He found, however, that giving a little here and there to each cultural strain was unworkable, largely because the forces of tradition violently stood up against change that threatened their power. Political exigency forced Haile Selassie to own up to this contradiction and to throw his support to the landed nobility. He may not have wanted to do this but he had to. Thus he did not succeed in fully resolving the contradiction; he merely accommodated himself to reality. He was still culturally divided even though he took a position on the issue. This would become evident in 1967 when for the last time in his life he made a tremendous effort to delimit the power of the feudal elite, and he failed. But the land tax and income tax programs, the new constitution, the establishment of a university system, and the opening of the Haile Selassie I Military Academy in Harar in 1958 to train the Imperial Bodyguard, were efforts made to position himself to the left, yet in the final analysis almost all these institutions were successfully used by the right. Since the latter were powerful and threatening to him, he stood with them as it was clear he could not destroy them. But he was unhappy with this position, indicating that his desire was to ally himself with modern forces. *Ras* Makonnen had succeeded in truly socializing Haile Selassie into accepting Western norms as having primary value. His acceptance of traditional norms arose from political need, but it was tangential. Over and over again his speeches during this period laid heavy stress on modernization.[29] It was clearly a stance he preferred but could not possibly opt for at this moment. Haile Selassie was no longer a prisoner of two cultures; he leaned heavily towards one but had to temporarily accept the other.

There was, however, never any irresolution when it came to a direct threat to Haile Selassie's position. He never hesitated to move rapidly to squash both the threat and its leaders. He would never abide the destruction of his control over Ethiopia and would never permit others to wield control over him. This hit too close to home as it brought back all the personages of the past—his mother and father, Empress Taitu and Empress Zauditu, Lij Yasu, *Fitwarari* Habte Giorgis, and Mussolini— who had caused in him such fear, helplessness, and anxiety.

When the Gojami notable Bitwoded Negash Bezebe conspired with others in 1951 to oust the emperor from power, he was quickly arrested and jailed for life. Many of his co-conspirators were flogged and subsequently jailed and their property confiscated by the emperor.

Another who incurred Haile Selassie's wrath was his close ally and, since 1941, Minister of the Pen, Wolde Giorgis Wolde Yohannes. Acting as the imperial secretariat, Wolde Giorgis

Haile Selassie, a few days prior to his coronation in 1930.
(Wide World Photos)

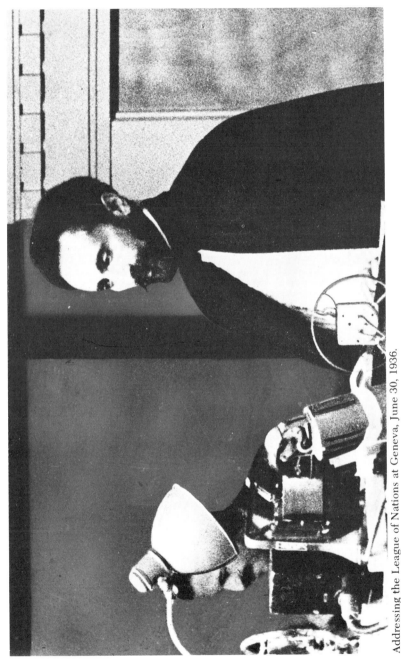

Addressing the League of Nations at Geneva, June 30, 1936.
(Wide World Photos)

The Lion of Judah and the Empress, as painted by an Ethiopian artist.
(Photograph by Elizabeth Sacre and Michael Freund)
From the author's private collection.

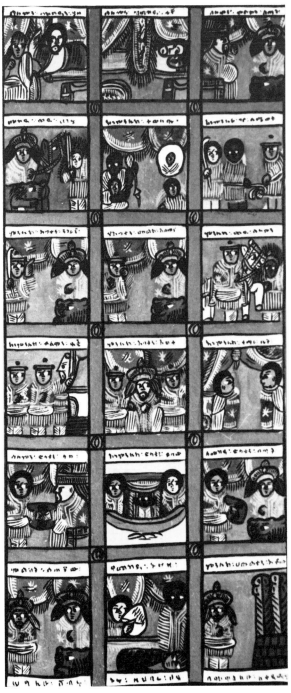

An Ethiopian artist's interpretation of the story of Solomon and Sheba.
(Photograph by Elizabeth Sacre and Michael Freund)
From the author's private collection.

ETHIOPIA

Alongside Liberian president, William Tubman, 1963.

Haile Selassie walking in the funeral procession for President John F. Kennedy. The second on the left is former French president Charles de Gaulle; on the emperor's right is King Baudouin of Belgium.

THE HORN OF AFRICA

Emperor Haile Selassie, 1962.

The Emperor with Kwame Nkrumah, President of Ghana, 1963. Behind Haile Selassie, on his left, is Crown Prince Asfa Wossen.

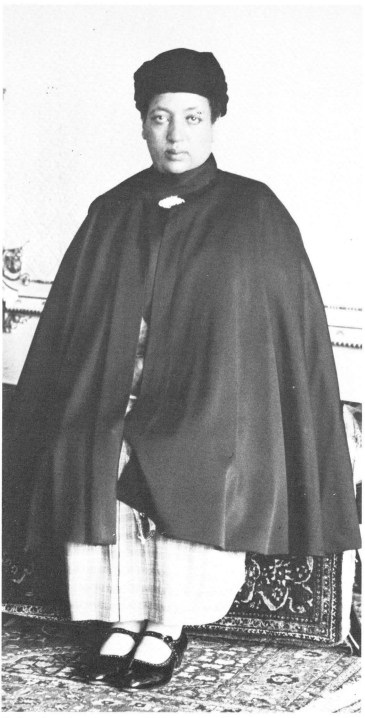

Haile Selassie's wife, Empress Woizero Menen, 1936.
(Wide World Photos)

Haile Selassie early in his reign.

was the second most powerful man in the country after the emperor. Following the emperor into exile and acting as his personal secretary in Bath, he had returned to Ethiopia with Haile Selassie in 1941, and since that time had had almost unrestricted access to the emperor. With such authority he became a feared man in both traditional and modern circles. Empress Menen and the crown prince, Asfa Wossen, feared he would intrigue to secure succession to the throne, while modern elements resented his tremendous efforts to prevent any of their plans from reaching fruition. Influenced by the strongest forces in the country, Haile Selassie became convinced that his comrade was a threat to his position. He was removed from Addis Ababa in 1955, losing all his national positions and was demoted to governor-general of Arussi Province, close enough to Shoa Province that he could be watched but far from the levers of national power. When informed by the emperor of his demotion, Wolde Giorgis "bowed low and made no comment, for he knew he would have been arrested if he had."[30]

Haile Selassie acted against both Bitwoded Negash Bezebe and Wolde Giorgis Wolde Yohannes as he would have liked to have acted against those who had prevented him from acquiring control of himself in the past. Both were present images of past ogres who had so victimized Haile Selassie. Both were excluded from his presence and removed from power in ways similar to the manner in which Haile Selassie would have operated in the past when he had felt out of control of life events, as when his parents died.

Without question Haile Selassie's roots affected his political behavior in this era. He attempted to resolve the cultural dualism to which he was exposed by his father, and the pattern by which he struck at his enemies at this time was similar to his earlier participation in actions against Taitu and *Ras* Gugsa. Little quarter was granted to those directly threatening the position and life of the emperor when power was available to him; the same pattern would be followed by Haile Selassie in his dealings with civil and revolutionary activity, and foreign threats.

9. The Horn of Africa and the American Connection

The Horn of Africa, an area on the east coast including Ethiopia, Somalia, and Djibouti, is an area of the world whose strategic location has thrust it into the international arena. Close to the Middle East and the Indian Ocean, it flanks the oil-rich states of Arabia, controls the Bab el Mandeb Straits, one of the narrow arteries of Israel's lifeline (a "chokepoint," William H. Lewis calls it[1]), dominates an area of the Gulf of Aden and of the Indian Ocean through which oil tankers are constantly moving, and overlooks the passage at which the Red Sea, the Gulf of Aden, and the Indian Ocean converge. It is a major geopolitical area of the world.

In 1953, at a time when neither Somalia nor Djibouti were independent, the United States signed a mutual-defense treaty with Ethiopia and laid the basis for the modernization of the Ethiopian military, which was to be used "exclusively to maintain [Ethiopia's] internal security, its legitimate self-defense, or to permit it to participate in the defense of the area."[2]

The defense treaty was part of the worldwide expansion of United States interests initiated by President Truman through the Truman Doctrine. The post–World War II era was dominated by the Cold War in which the Soviet Union and the United States were staking out political and military positions throughout the world. After the British withdrawal from their World War II occupation of Ethiopia, the United States realized the vulnerability of the area around the Horn of Africa and moved quickly to fill the vacuum. As Markakis has emphasized:

As in many other parts of the world, United States involvement
follow[ed] the retreat of British power in the postwar period. When
the British . . . were withdrawn . . . in 1951, they were replaced
with Americans. In return, Ethiopia . . . received military and economic assistance continuously. . . . At the end of [the 1960s]
Ethiopia was receiving 60% of all U.S. military aid supplies
for Africa. Generous U.S. assistance . . . enabled Ethiopia to
maintain a very large army by African standards.[3]

From 1953 to 1963 the United States provided Ethiopia with
$74 million in military assistance. By the end of Haile Selas-
sie's reign in 1974 this figure had reached $200 million, which
was then half the United States military assistance provided to
all African states.[4]

In pursuit of his own military and political objectives Haile
Selassie utilized America's fears of the Soviet Union to construct a military arsenal of extremely large proportions. Military weapons supplied to Ethiopia were utilized to fend off
domestic opponents, to obtain and hold on to Eritrea, to prevent Somali incursions into newly acquired Ethiopian territory in the Ogaden, and to maintain access to the port of
Djibouti. In addition, the armed forces built from American
funds secured the emperor's political position.

Traditional American military strategy as it applied to the
Indian Ocean and Red Sea was best articulated by Adm. Stansfield Turner, Director of the United States Central Intelligence Agency (CIA). He maintained that "the fundamental
role of our navy has been sea control. . . . The capability to
assist one's own use of the seas and to deny that use to others.
There are fundamentally two threats that the presence of a
naval force can imply: to do harm to a nation by projecting
power directly onto its territory or to sever a nation's sea lines
of communication through blockade or sea denial."[5]

A more specific statement regarding United States strategy
was put forward by former Defense Secretary James R.
Schlesinger. "The Soviet Union has become a major sea
power . . . in the [1960s]. The level of U.S. presence in the
Indian Ocean has been prudent. Since an effective military
balance is essential to the preservation of regional security
and stability in this area of great importance to the economic
well-being of the industrialized world, we feel we should
have logistical facilities which will permit us to maintain a

credible presence. In a period of historical transition toward a new set of power relations, only the United States among the Western nations has the stature to insure that the balance is maintained."[6]

The past two decades of American foreign policy on the Horn of Africa and the Indian Ocean was defined through these two policy statements. In effect a strong American presence on the Red Sea and Indian Ocean was perceived as absolutely necessary if (1) the economic security of the West was to be maintained, (2) stability and regional security were to be upheld in the Middle East and the Horn of Africa, (3) a potential blockade of Western oil lanes by the Soviets was to be prevented, and (4) the Red Sea and Indian Ocean were to be kept open for Israel and Israeli-bound shipping. The key to all this was the maintenance of a powerful and dominant American presence in the Indian Ocean. This policy was stated most succinctly by *The Wall Street Journal.* Through the lower end of the Red Sea and the Horn of Africa "passes all the Persian Gulf oil moving to the U.S., Western Europe, and Israel. All Suez Canal traffic to and from the Indian Ocean must pass the narrow strait of Bab el Mandeb between Djibouti and the two Yemens. Super tanker traffic heading for Africa's southern tip rides off the Somali coast. Whoever controls this area controls the oil flow to the Western world."[7]

In support of United States policy objectives a United States Military Assistance Advisory Group (MAAG) was attached to the Ethiopian Ministry of Defense in 1953, and in the same year Kagnew, an American base, was opened near Asmara, Eritrea, the most northern province of Ethiopia. It eventually quartered thirty-two hundred of the six thousand United States military personnel in Ethiopia.[8] Its functions included tracking satellites, monitoring communications, and allowing United States military forces access to the Red Sea.[9] Haile Selassie received weapons and huge amounts of military aid from the United States to construct a military that would reinforce his power, and in return the United States established a formidable military presence that would last until 1974. During the height of the Cold War in the 1950s and 1960s America was thus able to prevent the Soviet Union from playing an active role in the Red Sea.

The Ethiopian military under Haile Selassie was largely constructed by the United States, and all of its infrastructure was supplied by the United States. The Ethiopian army comprised forty thousand soldiers, the air force twenty-five hundred men, the navy two thousand troops, and the police had a thirty-thousand-man force. This was an extensive military for a country that in the 1950s and early 1960s was relatively immune from external attack. Throughout this time it was basically used in operations against domestic disorder, particularly in Gojam and Eritrea.

The American presence became even more formidable after 1962 when the Eritrean Liberation Front (ELF) organized its secessionist movement. Eritrea, proclaimed an Italian colony in the late nineteenth century, was occupied by England in 1941 during World War II. After the war, under terms of a resolution passed by the United Nations in 1952, Eritrea was federated with Ethiopia but retained a semi-autonomous status. This permitted Ethiopia access to the Red Sea as Eritrea included the ports of Massawa and Assab. The federation was part of Haile Selassie's policy of obtaining outlets to the sea that would be secure and dependable.[10] After 1960, when former Italian and British Somaliland were united to form the independent Somali Republic, Haile Selassie moved to incorporate Eritrea into Ethiopia. His fear was that Somalia, which had traditionally claimed the port of Djibouti as its own, might move to throw out the French colonial presence from Djibouti. This would disallow Ethiopian use of the port of Djibouti, through which a number of Ethiopian imports and exports flowed, making Ethiopia totally dependent upon Massawa and Assab. In 1962 Haile Selassie forced the Eritrean Assembly to vote itself out of existence and Eritrea was fully incorporated into Ethiopia as its fourteenth province.

Eritrea, 40 percent Muslim, was alien to Ethiopian culture which was dominated by the Christian Ethiopian Orthodox Church. In addition, the Italians had bred a political system in Eritrea that allowed Eritreans to incorporate internal self-government. Far more advanced industrially, politically, and alien culturally, the more radical Eritreans bridled at what was termed by them Ethiopian imperialism. In 1962 the Eritrean

Liberation Front (ELF), which had been set up in the 1950s, organized an army in an attempt to secede from Ethiopia. A Marxist group, the Eritrean Peoples' Liberation Front (EPLF), organized its own force in the 1960s, eventually joining in a temporary marriage with the ELF to expel the Ethiopians.

When the secessionist battle began in 1962, the United States sent in counterinsurgent teams, increased its military aid programs, and expanded its modernization and training program for the Ethiopian military. An extensive air force was also created with United States vintage jets.[11] At the same time Israel, fearful of a Muslim Eritrea that might act with other Muslim–Arab states to close off the Red Sea, initiated its own aid program in Ethiopia. Ethiopian commando units and security personnel were trained by the Israelis and they established for the Ethiopians a communications network in Eritrea that enabled the Ethiopian military to be more effective in its military operations in that province.[12] Until the overthrow of Haile Selassie, the United States, Israel, and Ethiopia were more or less allied in a common fight against the Eritrean Liberation Front. The United States viewed its national security interests in the Red Sea at stake, Israel was frightened of being cut off from access to the Red Sea, and Ethiopia feared the dismembering of its country and the loss of its newly acquired Red Sea ports.

Somalia, which became independent July 1, 1960, was an immediate and imminent threat to Ethiopia. The Ogaden region of Ethiopia has traditionally been held by Somalia to be part of its own territory. In 1948 Haile Selassie, with British concurrence, reoccupied the Ogaden, which had originally been taken by Menelik II, and later absorbed into the Italian empire, setting in motion the military and political hostilities that have existed between Ethiopia and Somalia since 1960. The coming of independence to Somalia brought with it traditional claims to the annexed Ogaden. The Somalis have pursued an irredentist policy towards the Ogaden by claiming that the area is populated by Islamic nomadic Somalis, and since Somalia recognizes the unity of its people, within the context of religion, language, and ethnicity, it became official policy to claim this land from Ethiopia. David D. Laitin's analysis of the Somali claims is precise.

Unlike all the new states of Africa, Somalia was a "nation" before it became a state. Some four million people inhabit the Horn of Africa, and they share a common language, a common religion, a common culture, and notably . . . a common understanding of themselves as a long-standing political community. In the early 1960s, therefore, when most African states were attempting a strategy of "nation-building"—the creation of a new identity consistent with their former colonial boundaries—Somalia could engage in "state-building," or the enhancement of political control at the new centre. Further, the Somalis were unique in Africa in that they had multi-irredentist claims. The five-pointed star on their flag represents the Northern and Southern regions of the present Republic, as well as the "unredeemed" Northeastern province of Kenya, the Ogaden province of Ethiopia, and the French territory of Afars and Issas [Djibouti]. These three political entities are largely Somali in population.[13]

In the mid-1960s American military aid to Ethiopia was sharply increased as it became clear to American policymakers that the Soviet Union was increasing its aid to Somalia. Initial military assistance agreements between the civilian government of Somalia and the Soviet Union, calling for $35 million in grants and credits, were signed in 1963. After 1969 when the civilian government of Somalia was overthrown by the armed forces, General Maxamed Siyad Barre, heading the "socialist" Supreme Revolutionary Council, developed Somalia's connection with Russia, and by 1971, $50 million in grants had been approved by the Soviets. Additionally, in 1962 the Soviet Union began assisting Somalia in constructing port facilities in Berbera, overlooking the Red Sea. The facilities were completed in 1969. Naval support networks including two Soviet communication facilities were opened in Berbera in 1972, and the Soviet air base was opened at Harghessa the same year. By 1977 Russia had granted more than $250 million in military aid to Somalia.[14] According to J. Bowyer Bell, there were "some 2,000 Soviet personnel in Somalia including 300 military advisors."[15] Former Defense Secretary James Schlesinger claims the Soviets established a missile storage and handling facility at Berbera.

There is some question as to how extensive these facilities at Berbera actually were. Yet, insofar as American policymaking is concerned, the perception is as important as the reality and all major United States government authorities seemed to agree that they were extensive enough to be threatening to American interests in the Red Sea area.

The harbor at Berbera is almost directly across from the
Soviet naval facilities in South Yemen's port of Aden. This had
obvious strategic benefits for the Soviet Union. Utilizing these
harbors for shipping and docking altered to some degree the
balance of power in the Indian Ocean/Red Sea/Gulf of Aden
area. It was possible to choke off Israel; and it was possible to
dominate the seas through which oil passes to the Western
industrial states. American policy, predicated on retaining its
position on the Horn of Africa, maintaining the lifeline to
Israel, and preventing a *potential* blockade of Western oil
lanes, had clearly received a setback. Utilizing South Yemen
and Somalia, the Soviets succeeded by the mid-1970s in af-
fecting the balance of power off the Horn of Africa in their
favor.

Throughout this period Haile Selassie gained immeasurable
strength via the American alliance. With Ethiopia concerned
about Somali aggression, and the United States fearful of
Soviet intentions on the Red Sea via its influence in Somalia,
both countries opposed the Somalia–Soviet connection.
Ethiopia maintained a garrison of some ten thousand troops
in the Ogaden to fend off Somali attacks, while the United
States enlarged upon its own presence in Ethiopia and tried to
shore up, even more than it already had, the Ethiopian armed
forces. The United States was so firmly committed to the
security of the Haile Selassie regime that it secretly agreed to
"reaffirm its continuing interest in the security of Ethiopia and
its opposition to any activities threatening the territorial integrity of Ethiopia."[16] Playing on the Cold War between Russia
and the United States, Haile Selassie received the military
wherewithal to build a military that was one of the largest and
best-trained in Africa.

Massawa and Assab, the two Red Sea ports deep within
Eritrea, are the only outlets to the sea that Ethiopia has access
to within its own territory. Djibouti, a largely Muslim state
which received its independence from France in 1977, three
years after the ouster of Haile Selassie, offered another avenue
to the sea. A railroad line between Addis Ababa and the port at
Djibouti has existed since 1917. Since the 1960s when the war
with Eritrea became intense, some 40 percent–60 percent of
Ethiopia's exports and imports have flowed through the port at

Djibouti, although this avenue was periodically curtailed due
to insurgent Somali activity in which the railroad line was often
severed.

Insofar as foreign and domestic policy is concerned,
Ethiopia has, since 1962 when it annexed Eritrea, viewed
with one lens the crisis in Eritrea, Somali independence, and
its relationship with French Djibouti. When the Eritrean Liberation Movement began its secessionist war in 1962, Haile
Selassie reacted by sending in armed forces. There was to be
no consideration of separatist demands for independence. As
the Ethiopian–Eritrean war increased in scope and violence,
the military was reinforced and by 1965 some 50 percent of the
Ethiopian army, twenty thousand troops, were stationed or
fighting in Eritrea. United States and Israeli military aid was
increased.

Throughout this period Haile Selassie placed pressure on
France to remain in Djibouti. With France removed as a colonial power Djibouti would be at the mercy of Somalia which
consistently claimed it as part of its territory. With the war in
Eritrea, with increasing border problems with the Sudan re-
sulting from the flow of refugees from Eritrea, with Sudanese
accusations that the war was spilling over onto its territory,
with internal rebellion in 1967 in Gojam Province, and with
the then intermittent war with Somalia over the Ogaden,
Ethiopia was in no position to contend with an independent
state of Djibouti. And dealing with Djibouti meant a potential
full-scale war with Somalia. It had been policy under Haile
Selassie not to permit Somalia control over Djibouti as
Ethiopia would then be totally dependent upon Assab and
Massawa, and with the secessionist war raging, such dependence was intolerable to Ethiopia's national interest.

From 1953 to 1974 the emperor maintained close ties with
the United States. After 1974 the alliance fell apart as Haile
Selassie himself was deposed in the swirl of a military coup
and the United States decided to leave its base in Asmara and
move to Diego Garcia, an island fifteen hundred miles off the
coast of Africa and safe from the turmoil on the Horn.[17] In
effect Haile Selassie was abandoned by America because of its
desire to secure its national interests on the Horn from a more
secure geographic position. But in the twenty-year period

beginning in 1953, the United States and Ethiopia constructed a containment policy that had regional and international implications. Haile Selassie was able to prevent Eritrean secession, and because of him the ELF/EPLF was unable to fully effect its policy. Somalia was kept out of the Ogaden throughout the entire period of the emperor's rule. Not until 1977, with huge support from the Soviet Union, did Somalia temporarily occupy the Ogaden. In early 1978 the Somalis were thrown out by the Ethiopians and the Soviet Union, the latter in 1977 shifting its alliance to Ethiopia after having been thrown out of Somalia. But Haile Selassie had kept Somalia in check. Djibouti too was kept secure for Ethiopian exports and imports.[18]

The foreign policy constructed by Haile Selassie after the departure of the British worked to the emperor's advantage, at least in the short run. The military buildup, which completely secured the emperor's throne until the mid-1970s, did, however, contain the seeds for the coup that would finally remove Haile Selassie from power. But for the moment the new military served Haile Selassie well. It allowed him to exert control over secessionist and foreign forces trying to weaken his authority; it permitted Ethiopian expansion into the Ogaden and Eritrea, which created the geographic boundaries of Ethiopia that still exist and which tied Haile Selassie to the empire builders of Ethiopia's imperial past; it created the circumstances by which Haile Selassie one last time tried to destroy the power of feudalism; and it presented him to the world as a modern leader who had control over an efficient and wieldy military machine. The American connection was used well and was of enormous benefit to Haile Selassie.

Although Haile Selassie and Ethiopia were extraordinarily dependent upon the United States, the emperor tried exceedingly hard to diversify his international donors in an attempt to reduce America's influence and authority over him. Throughout this period Haile Selassie traveled extensively to Europe, Asia, the Middle East, Africa, and the United States. Using his international prestige and his domestic position, he lobbied states to support him in his policies in Somalia, Eritrea, and Djibouti. His efforts were rewarded as Muslim and Arab states held their financial support of Eritrea in check even though they had every reason to fully support secession, particularly

Saudi Arabia which was intent on improving its status on the
Red Sea and limiting the Soviet penetration there. The African
members of the Organization of African Unity (OAU) refused
to support Somali interests in the Ogaden, and the Soviet
Union too held Somalia back from invading the Ogaden even
though it was its prime military backer. Haile Selassie was
masterful in neutralizing support for his opponents in Eritrea
and Somalia. The failure of the military junta that overthrew
the emperor to successfully continue this policy lends credence to the argument that Haile Selassie's influence over
other world leaders was large.

The emperor also diversified sources of economic aid.
Yugoslavia, Sweden, the Soviet Union, the People's Republic
of China, Taiwan, Italy, and West Germany were major
suppliers of aid, grants, and skilled labor. Although these
states never approached the influence generated in Ethiopia
by the United States, Haile Selassie achieved some international maneuverability by tying Ethiopia to states other than
America.

The United States however was the major military donor
and knew it, and although Haile Selassie benefited from the
relationship, the United States was the primary force behind
Haile Selassie's power, and he knew that. It did not prevent
him, however, from achieving his goals and to that extent
Haile Selassie was firmly behind American policy on the Horn
of Africa. Both he and the United States retained control of the
Horn area, at least until 1974, and thus the emperor can be
said to have succeeded in achieving his goals as he saw them
in 1953 when the American–Ethiopian alliance began. He was
secure on the throne, he maintained Eritrea and the Ogaden as
part of Ethiopia, and he now had a military that was potent.
Haile Selassie and Ethiopia were clients of the United States
but that did not prevent the emperor from arranging the relationship in such a way as to suit himself. He was thus satisfied
and pleased with the pact for it allowed him to retain control of
Ethiopia.

10. A Man of Africa

Having had a taste of international prestige during the Italian-Ethiopian crisis of the 1930s, and unsatisfied with being merely a man of Ethiopia, Haile Selassie over the years successfully sought a dominant position among leaders in Africa. The primary motivation for his activity within Africa was the political threat he felt by the emergence of Ghana as an independent state in 1957 and particularly its prime minister, Kwame Nkrumah. Nkrumah, perceiving himself a radical of the left intent on eliminating Western colonial influences, was certainly seen by Haile Selassie and other political conservatives as a threat to their own power. Haile Selassie was deeply embedded in a military relationship with the United States, but even more important, he looked to the West for economic, political, and personal support. Without the military weapons received from the United States, it was unlikely that Haile Selassie could have maintained himself on the throne. Half of all United States military assistance to Africa was channeled to Ethiopia, and Kagnew, the American military base near Asmara, quartered some thirty-two hundred of the six thousand U.S. military personnel stationed in Ethiopia. What is more, the United States had a mutual security agreement with Ethiopia, and with the exception of a similar pact with Liberia, the only arrangement of its kind in Africa, whereby the "United States Government . . . reaffirm[ed] . . . its opposition to any activities threatening the territorial integrity of Ethiopia."[1] The emperor was particularly frightened of Ghanaian support of the Eritrean secessionists.

Moreover Haile Selassie had always considered himself the majordomo of Africa whereas the prestige attached to being the leader of the first nation to obtain its independence from European imperialism afforded Nkrumah the opportunity to become a dominant presence in Africa. Haile Selassie was more than irked, he felt threatened. It is noteworthy to recall that Haile Selassie's acute involvement in overall African affairs did not begin until 1958, just one year after Ghana received its independence from Great Britain.

Prior to this time Ethiopia and Liberia were the primary African states. Although both countries had had their difficulties with more powerful European nations, neither had been colonized and both Haile Selassie and Liberian President William Tubman were considered primary spokesmen for Africa. It was a role both relished but usually avoided, as in Liberia, Tubman was intent on securing his position and that of the American-Liberian elite that supported him, while Haile Selassie was busy centralizing his political authority and increasing his personal power within Ethiopia. Since both leaders took for granted their continental leadership roles, neither saw any personal or political need to functionally take up the mantle and speak out against European colonialism that had African territories under its control from the sixteenth century onward. Liberia was the only other African territory that had a mutual security pact with the United States, but more than that, the U.S. had traditionally been the guarantor of Liberian independence—a role it had played since 1846. Tubman and Haile Selassie saw no gain in opposing Western interests as their national and personal interests required them to do otherwise. Both remained silent in the face of colonialism in Africa, and recognized a real challenge in 1957 when Nkrumah began pressuring Europe to pull out of Africa. Nkrumah took upon himself the mantle of spokesman of Africa, and was severely critical of Ethiopia and Liberia for not doing so earlier. Haile Selassie knew then that he could no longer isolate himself from African affairs. There was a threat to prestige, a political threat, and a personal threat to the control he so wanted, and wanted even more desperately when he was challenged.

The personal element was the primary motivating factor that propelled Haile Selassie into the forefront of African politics. And the key personal variable was the issue of control. He felt once again the anxiety of being at the mercy of external forces, believed that he was back at Menelik's palace, on the Ethiopian front battling the Italians, or temporarily out of power in 1960. This time the feeling was less acute because it was not so close to home but those feelings nevertheless emerged, and with them came anger, anxiety, and depression. While the emperor fled from political impotence in 1936, he decided this time to battle Nkrumah for dominance much as he fought in 1960. He could afford the luxury of this decision; since the immediate threat was less the anxiety was reduced.

Once the decision to fight was made Haile Selassie moved into the fray with relish. Not only did he believe he could win but he was back in a comfortable role and one that he enjoyed. Other African states were soon due to become independent and Haile Selassie was to find himself again in the company of heads of state, the pioneering leaders of independent Africa. He had been so successful in Geneva in 1936 that he had full confidence in his ability to sway this new leadership. He also saw the forthcoming political battle as the opportunity to create a historical niche for himself. Already an international statesman, and the emperor of Ethiopia, he could now close the circle and generate an image as leader of Africa. He knew that his future in history depended more on his international position than it did on his control of Ethiopia, and emerging as an African spokesman would clearly be the vehicle that would, along with Geneva, carry him into the pages of history.

So, even though the struggle for power was in large measure predicated on personal anxiety, Haile Selassie still looked forward to doing battle with Nkrumah. Not only could it bring psychological rewards and a strengthening of his personal identity but it would vastly improve his international image by reinforcing the stature he acquired in Geneva. He looked upon this political struggle with mixed feelings because he was motivated by different forces. But he thought surely he could win, as he always had in the past, and the security of past successes unquestionably determined his decision in this matter. He would let nothing stand in his way and he had every intention of emerging from this diplomatic foray victorious and secure.

In April 1958 Haile Selassie made his first major speech on African unity, tying Ethiopia's struggle against Italy to African independence from its colonial overlords.

> The world is only now coming to realize what Ethiopia and Africa have long recognized, that peace, independence, and the prosperity of mankind can be achieved and assured only by the collective and united efforts of free men who are prepared to maintain eternal vigilance and labour unceasingly to protect those most precious of God's gifts. The sympathy and support which Ethiopia received from other African peoples when she was invaded twenty-three years ago is ample testimony of the strong sentiments which unite all free African countries. . . . Ethiopia knows that the willingness of the Independent States of Africa to co-operate and work together in solving their common problems and achieving their common goals is essential to the continued progress of the African peoples.[2]

Presented at the First Conference of Independent African States which was held in Accra, Ghana, the speech symbolized Haile Selassie's entrance into the pan-African movement. The participating states included Ghana, Liberia, Ethiopia, Egypt, Tunisia, Libya, Sudan, and Morocco, and they committed themselves to securing the emancipation of the continent—declaring a diplomatic war on colonialism. The conference represented for Haile Selassie the end of his isolation from African affairs and the beginning of his role as a moderate in Pan-African councils. A major plank of this Conference of Independent States was the agreement that all states would agree to observe each other's territorial and political integrity. With Eritrea in mind, Haile Selassie was more than delighted with this statement of principle.[3]

With the establishment of a loose regional union of Ghana, Guinea, and Mali in 1960, a polemic between Nkrumah and Haile Selassie began in earnest. All three states mentioned were politically radical and in Haile Selassie's opinion Marxist in ideology; thus they were considered by him to be extraordinarily threatening to his position in Africa. Kwame Nkrumah and Sekou Toure, the president of Guinea, politically aligned themselves with the Soviet Union and aggressively pushed a program calling for the political unification of Africa under one ruler. This radical approach to Pan-

Africanism was markedly at variance with Haile Selassie's position which foresaw the creation of mechanisms that would allow African states to harmonize their economies but would leave aside any political arrangements among independent African states. This division would grow to major proportions and would place Haile Selassie and Nkrumah in direct opposition to one another.

With moderates led by Tubman and Haile Selassie calling for African unity based on economic affairs within a very loose, almost nonexistent political community, and radicals led by Nkrumah and Toure demanding a political union of all African states, a Second Conference of Independent African States was called in 1960 to try to resolve the issue. The meeting was held in Addis Ababa, the Ethiopian capital. Nothing was resolved. But from this point on events moved rapidly. Nigeria, the most populous country in Africa, gained its independence from Britain in 1960 and France granted independence that same year to thirteen former African territories. Civil and ethnic war erupted in the former Belgian Congo in 1960, and during the course of the war Prime Minister Patrice Lumumba, whom Nkrumah strongly supported, was assassinated. The United Nations sent its armed forces into the Congo (presently known as Zaire) to quell the civil war, and the United States intruded into the war supporting the conservative elements who were opposed to the more radical Lumumba. Moderates and radicals within Africa took altogether different sides in the dispute.[4]

The ideological and political divisions were institutionalized in regional African charters in 1961. In January, Morocco, Ghana, Guinea, Mali, Egypt, Libya, and the Algerian Provisional Government met in Casablanca, Morocco, and proclaimed their determination "to promote the triumph of liberty all over Africa and to achieve [Africa's political] unity."[5] For the first time an African conference was held that restricted its participants to those sharing similar ideology.

The more conservative states met four months later in Monrovia, Liberia. Congo (Brazzaville), the Ivory Coast, Madagascar, Cameroun, Chad, Gabon, the Central African Republic, Dahomey, Niger, Upper Volta, Mauritania, Senegal, Liberia, Nigeria, Somalia, Sierra Leone, Togo, Libya, and Ethiopia attended the meeting. The Monrovia resolution on the question of African unity and continental leadership was in direct contrast with the Casablanca resolution.

> The unity that is aimed to be achieved at the moment is not the political integration of sovereign African states, but unity of aspirations and of action considered from the point of view of African social solidarity and political identity.[6]

According to Colin Legum,

> the general attitude of the Monrovians is reformist . . . rather than revolutionary. . . . Their chief preoccupation is with their own affairs; they are not champions of a political concept which they would like to persuade *all* the African states to adopt.[7]

Conservatives and radicals also differed sharply over the issue of non-alignment—that each state express freely its opinions on matters of international importance but it must not make alliances with either Russia or the United States. Nkrumah advocated an aggressive, largely anti-Western approach and he and the radicals were often found supporting the Soviet Union, while Haile Selassie and the more moderate and conservative elements in Africa were usually found in the Western camp. Political ideology was the variable that created the gap between the two blocs, and Marxism as conceived by Nkrumah became the weaponry of battles fought at future conferences between those countries professing it and those other countries such as Ethiopia which were ideologically or politically allied with the Western democracies. For example, Nkrumah could proceed from words such as these (from his *Handbook of Revolutionary Warfare*):

> A state can be said to be a neo-colonialist or client state if it is independent de jure and dependent de facto. It is a state where political power lies in the conservative forces of the former colony and where economic power remains under the control of international finance capital.[8]

However correct Nkrumah may have been about such matters the quotation describes, it was his political perceptiveness that so rattled his ideological opponents and forced them to sharpen their opposition to him. A dominant charismatic force, Nkrumah appeared to be gaining the upper hand in his debate with Haile Selassie and Tubman, and the emperor decided that he would have to use all his diplomatic prowess if he were to emerge victorious from this ideological battle.

In 1962 Haile Selassie invited the leaders of all independent African states to a summit conference to be held in Addis Ababa the following year. The expressed purpose of the conference was to resolve the issue of African unity, but primarily the emperor, by holding the conference in Ethiopia, had every intention of outmaneuvering Nkrumah and seeing to it that his own interpretation of unity received delegate acceptance. At the 1962 Conference of Independent States held at Lagos, Nigeria, Haile Selassie discussed the reasoning behind his invitation.

> We are told that Africa has been split into competing groups and that this is inhibiting cooperation among the African states and severely retarding African progress. . . . Ethiopia considers herself a member of one group only—the African group. . . . When we Africans have been misled into pigeonholing one another, into attributing rigid and inflexible views to states which were present at one conference but not at another, then we shall, without reason or justification, have limited our freedom of action and rendered immeasurably more difficult the task of joining our efforts, in harmony and brotherhood, in the common cause of Africa.[9]

The emperor had developed a strategy to defeat Nkrumah that politically could not be questioned and it was a marvelous example of diplomatic dexterity. Heretofore Haile Selassie had been identified as opposing Nkrumah's philosophy, and since Nkrumah appeared to be gaining adherents, to the dismay of the emperor, Haile Selassie shifted his ground and positioned himself in dead center. Although he maintained his conservative stance, being set against radicalism of any kind, Haile Selassie now appeared to African leaders in the role of conciliator. He would act as a mediator and bring the opposing schools of thought together. Should this policy meet with success all credit would flow to him and he would thereby completely circumvent Nkrumah and in the process attain an extraordinary amount of stature in Africa. Not only did this strategy work; it functioned with such precision that from 1963 on, Haile Selassie was considered the preeminent African statesman, first among equals.

The summit meeting of African states opened May 22, 1963, in Addis Ababa. Thirty of the thirty-two African states attended (only Togo and Morocco were absent), making this the largest continental conference of its kind ever held. As honorary president, Haile Selassie addressed the opening session.

We are meeting here today to lay the basis for African unity. Let us, here and now, agree upon the basic instrument which will constitute the foundation for the future growth . . . of this continent.

Africa's victory is not yet total, and areas of resistance still remain. Today we name as our first great task the final liberation of those Africans still dominated by foreign exploitation and control. . . . Our liberty is meaningless unless all Africans are free.

Let us also resolve that old wounds shall be healed and past scars forgotten. It was thus that Ethiopia treated the invader nearly twenty-five years ago, and Ethiopians found peace with honor in this course. . . . We must live in peace with our former colonizers, shunning recrimination and bitterness and forswearing the luxury of vengeance and re-taliation lest the acid of hatred erode our souls and poison our hearts. . . .

We look to the vision of Africa not merely free but united. . . . We know that there are differences among us. . . . But we also know that unity can be and has been attained among men of the most disparate origins. . . . We are determined to create a union of Africans.

But while we agree that the ultimate destiny of this continent lies in political union, we must at the same time recognize that the obstacles to be overcome in its achievement are numerous and for-midable. Africa's peoples did not emerge into liberty in uniform conditions. Africans maintain different political systems; our economies are diverse; our social orders are rooted in differing cul-tures and traditions. Further, no clear consensus exists on the "how" and the "what" of this union. Is it to be federal, confederal, or unitary? Is the sovereignty of individual states to be reduced, and, if so, by how much and in what areas?

We should therefore not be concerned that complete union is not attained from one day to the next. The union we seek can only come gradually as the day-to-day progress which we achieve carries us slowly but inexorably along this course. . . . Thus a period of transi-tion is inevitable.

There is, nonetheless, much we can do to speed this transition. Let us seize on . . . areas of agreement and . . . take action now. . . .[10]

Although many issues were discussed between May 22 and 26, the primary result of the conference, which added immea-surable luster to Haile Selassie's image, was the immediate establishment of the continental-wide Organization of African Unity (OAU). In order to promote unity and solidarity, to achieve a better life for Africans, to defend the sovereignty of Africa, to eradicate all forms of colonialism, and to promote international cooperation, the OAU Charter was signed and the Organization created. Four primary institutions were es-tablished to carry out its principles of sovereign equality, non-interference in the internal affairs of states, peaceful set-tlement of disputes, the emancipation of African territories still under colonial rule, and non-alignment.[11] The political and diplomatic importance of the Organization is clearly represented by the states adhering to the Charter and by the African leaders who signed the document in 1963:

Ahmed Ben Bella/Algeria, King Nwambudsa IV/Burundi, Ahmadou Ahidjo/Cameroun, David Dacko/Central African Republic, Francois Tombalbayne/Chad, Abbe Fulbert Youlou/Congo Brazzaville, Joseph Kasavubu/Congo Leopoldville, Hubert Maga/Dahomey, Haile Selassie/Ethiopia, Leon M'ba/Gabon, Kwame Nkrumah/Ghana, Sekou Toure/Guinea, Felix Houphouet-Boigny/Ivory Coast, William Tubman/Liberia, Hassan Mohammed Rida/Libya, Philibert Tsiranana/Madagascar, Modibo Keita/Mali, Mokhtar Ould Daddah/Mauritania, Hamani Diori/Niger, Abubakar Tafewa Balewa/Nigeria, Habemenshi/Rwanda, Leopold Senghor/Senegal, Milton Margai/Sierra Leone, Abdullah Osman/Somalia, Ibrahim Abboud/Sudan, Julius Nyerere/Tanganyika, Habib Bourguiba/Tunisia, Milton Obote/Uganda, Gamal Abdel Nasser/United Arab Republic, Maurice Yameogo/Upper Volta.

Morocco and Togo signed the Charter at a later date as have all other African states that have since become independent.

The Charter was largely of Haile Selassie's making and gave a little to each side in the dispute over unity. The promotion of unity, rather than the construction of it, was a victory for Haile Selassie and Tubman, as was the designation of the *official* name of the organization—the Organization of African and Malagasy States—which did not include the word *union*. The agreement of sovereignty for each country, and the unreserved condemnation of subversive activities carried out by African leaders against other African leaders were also victories for the conservative bloc. The desires of Nkrumah and his supporters were also recognized in the Charter. The statement calling for the eradication of colonialism *in all its forms* was a reference to neo-colonialism. The word *unity* was incorporated into the title of the Charter to pacify Nkrumah. The principle of *absolute dedication* to freeing remaining colonial territories implied the use of violence to achieve this result, something the moderates had previously opposed.

Both blocs had argued in the past that neutrality for Africa was necessary. But, they disagreed on its definition in that Nkrumah and Toure pushed for *positive neutrality,* which meant in effect that African states would make their views known in public forum and would often side first with one group, then with another on all international issues. The conservatives pushed for *non-alignment,* which, as they expressed it, meant that Africans could voice their opinions but should concentrate on issues surrounding Africa. The conservatives had a hard time swallowing the pill of positive neutrality, for it meant in practice a more leftist approach to foreign affairs, and most of the conservative states were politically, economically, and militarily tied to the West. In the Charter of the OAU (the pact has always been unofficially called the Organization of African Unity) the principle of non-alignment as it was stated appeared to be a victory for the conservatives but the expression of the principle was left purposely vague, giving free play to its interpretation. More then anything else, the Charter had Haile Selassie written all over it. Tubman and Nkrumah would leave Addis after the conclusion of the conference secure in the knowledge that each had contributed to the formulation of the Charter but both knew also that they had been overshadowed by the formidable emperor.

> The conference had several significant results. First, Haile Selassie eclipsed the more extreme leaders of Africa and gave the Pan-African movement a new and more moderate direction. Second, Ethiopia committed itself to Africa, thus ending its traditional isolation. . . . Third, the Ethiopian government had become an important spokesman for Africa.[12]

The strategy developed by Haile Selassie to delimit the impact of Nkrumah over other African leaders worked exceedingly well. The OAU charter was perceived by African heads of state as the fruition of Haile Selassie's efforts to bring closer cooperation among African nations on his terms. Julius Nyerere, the president of Tanzania, commented on the vitality and importance of the Charter, subtly applauding Haile Selassie's efforts and mocking Nkrumah.

> There will be some who will say that this Charter does not go far enough or that it is not revolutionary enough. This may be so. But what is going far enough? No good mason would complain that his first brick did not go far enough. He knows that a first brick will go as

far as it can go and no further. He will go on laying brick after brick until the edifice is complete. Some will think it is not revolutionary. A true revolutionary is not an unrealistic dreamer. A true revolutionary is one who analyzes any given situation with scientific objectivity and then acts accordingly. That is what this conference has been doing. Examining realistically what it is that we have in common in our approach to unity and then act accordingly.[13]

Haile Selassie had effectively undercut Nkrumah and in so doing acquired new prestige internationally and within Ethiopia. For those forces inside Ethiopia who had claimed that the emperor had permitted the country to fall behind other states in image had to admit that this was no longer so. Most important, however, Haile Selassie reinforced his own success at Geneva. Though Nkrumah was no Mussolini, in the emperor's mind, of course, the leader of Ghana represented an image that mirrored the Italian leader. Both were trying to amputate the emperor's power and authority and both were symbols of an even earlier time when Haile Selassie was effectively at the mercy of others, i.e., Empress Zauditu, and *Fitwarari* Habte Giorgis, the minister of war in the post–Menelik II era. Doing battle with Nkrumah was not so different, and the Ghanaian was seen through the emperor's distorted psyche as the image of all those who had opposed him in the past. There was no choice but to engage Nkrumah because Haile Selassie was not psychologically free to do anything else. When Haile Selassie had his back against the wall, he had always chosen either to run, manipulate, or fight. In this case he opted for the latter two options and, through diplomatic manipulation, defeated the charismatic and often bombastic Nkrumah.

Although Nkrumah continues to be thought of as the father of an indigenous Pan-Africanism, and rightfully so since he did so much to generate theoretical support for it, Haile Selassie, after 1963, was considered the elder statesman of Africa. He represented to many the true virtues of the continent; he had almost single-handedly created the OAU; he was a man of history, and he had put Nkrumah in his place when other statesmen were unable to. Haile Selassie had risen to the occasion and had brought a disparate group of political and ideological entities together under the roof of the OAU. It was a remarkable achievement. To honor the emperor for his ef-

forts, the headquarters of the OAU were established in Addis
Ababa. Besides having its own offices, Africa Hall, a gleaming
white building just across the street from Jubilee Palace, is
utilized to accommodate delegate meetings of the OAU. In the
center of its lobby is found the modern stained-glass window
painted by the most noted and important Ethiopian artist
Afewerk Tekle. As large as it is beautiful and stunning, it is a
representation of Ethiopia leading Africa to its future.

With the conclusion of the conference May 26, 1963, Haile
Selassie had become a man of Africa. Five years of direct
confrontation with the radicals of Africa and thirty-three years
as emperor of Ethiopia had brought him to this stage in life. It
was one of his happier moments, one that brought him tremendous gratification and a gentle feeling of contentment with
the fruits that life was offering him. Haile Selassie in 1964
stated that the establishment of the OAU, enabling Africans to
speak with one voice and to act in unison, was a momentous
occasion, "a supreme moment of great historical vision."[14]
There can be little doubt that he was primarily speaking of his
own vision, and for the emperor indeed it was a momentous
occasion of great personal satisfaction. The imagery of Addis
Ababa in 1963 was, in his own mind, almost comparable to the
imagery of Geneva in 1936. Yet, Haile Selassie was intent on
building upon this image. He took his role as mediator seriously, thus reinforcing his now symbolic position as elder
statesman of Africa. In divisions between Algeria and
Morocco, Ghana and Guinea, and among Nigerians in the
Nigeria/Biafra civil war, Haile Selassie played the role of conciliator, a role he was so successful at in 1963.

Algeria and Morocco commenced fighting in 1963 over a
disputed border area and were eventually brought to the
peace table through the efforts of Haile Selassie in his role as
leader of an arbitration committee established by the OAU.
The delegation, consisting of Ethiopia, the Ivory Coast, Mali,
Nigeria, Senegal, Sudan, and Tanganyika, brought the two
sides together at Bamako, Mali, where Morocco and Algeria
came to a negotiated settlement that was approved in Cairo in
1964 at the first Assembly of the OAU Heads of State.[15]

After the overthrow of Kwame Nkrumah by the Ghanaian
military in 1966, relations between Guinea, where Nkrumah

fled as honorary president, and the new government in Ghana became tense. Again, through the good offices of Haile Selassie, a provocative situation was dealt with and relations between the two disputants improved.[16] The irony of Haile Selassie's position in this dispute should not go unnoticed!

Haile Selassie was also chosen as chairman of an advisory mission established by the Organization of African Unity September 14, 1967, to express support for the territorial integrity, unity and peace of Nigeria during the civil war that followed Biafran secession from Nigeria in May 1967. Throughout the three years of this tragic and brutal war, Haile Selassie moved to end the conflict. His lack of success in this venture was partly due to the fact that he was no objective interloper in that he clearly supported Nigerian unity and therefore was quite unacceptable to Biafran leaders. Haile Selassie, who was facing his own secessionist movement in Eritrea, could not support Biafran secession because of its implications for Ethiopia. Constant attempts to solve the problem failed. Then in August 1968 Haile Selassie succeeded in bringing both sides to the negotiating table in Addis Ababa. The negotiations failed to result in an agreement. (There was similar failure in Monrovia in 1969 when the emperor and his mission oversaw talks between representatives of the warring parties.) The civil war did not end until 1970 when overpowering Nigerian forces caused the collapse of Biafra.[17]

Following the Biafran surrender, Haile Selassie was approached by Nigeria, and the four African states—Ivory Coast, Gabon, Tanzania, Zambia—that had recognized Biafra. They requested that he use his good offices to bring about a reconciliation. After several weeks of discussion and mediation, the emperor announced a rapprochement September 1, 1970.

As a Third World leader, Haile Selassie met periodically with President Tito of Yugoslavia. In 1967 both agreed that states in their mutual relations should be guided by the principles of peaceful coexistence and that these principles, widely accepted in non-aligned countries, contributed towards easing tension and furthering cooperation between states on the basis of mutual respect. Tito made Haile Selassie an honorary citizen of Yugoslavia in 1972 because of the emperor's efforts on behalf of Africa and the Third World.

So the emperor had once again combined the personal with the political and had achieved success in both domains. He emerged from the Addis Ababa meetings in 1963 a major force in Africa, truly earning the plaudits that were then heaped upon him. He was indeed a lion and never was this title more appropriate. He had lashed out at the radicals and had forced them to come to terms with him. He had established the framework upon which the OAU was constructed and in so doing had made Africa a force to be reckoned with in international circles. The OAU was his child and he and everyone else knew it. As the *New York Times* said editorially, the OAU "would never have come into existence at Addis Ababa in 1963 without the masterful diplomacy of Haile Selassie."[18]

When the Ethiopian junta which overthrew Haile Selassie in 1974 was thought to be contemplating his execution, many representatives in the United Nations interrupted a General Assembly discussion on the credentials of the Cambodian delegation to plead with the junta to spare the emperor's life. As one African leader said, "He belongs to Africa."[19] Haile Selassie had become an indelible African presence in 1963.

11. Haile Selassie as Father, Asfa Wossen as Son

The heir apparent to the throne, Crown Prince Asfa Wossen, has had a stormy relationship with his father, Haile Selassie, and has forever lived in the shadow of the emperor. "A quiet and apparently unassuming man, he spends much of his time with books and has a reputation [among the elite] of being remarkably well informed about literature and politics."[1] Born in 1916, the crown prince is a portly and sickly man who was felled by a stroke in 1974 and is presently living in exile in Switzerland. He is the sole surviving son of Haile Selassie and his wife Empress Menen, and is representative of the poor fortune the monarch had in the raising of his children.

Princess Zanabe Work, who was forced by the emperor to marry *Ras* Gugsa of Tigre when she was fourteen years old, died in 1933, one year after the marriage was consummated. Princess Tsahay died in 1942 when she was newly married and young, leaving no descendants. Only the eldest daughter, Princess Tenegne Work, who was born in 1913, survived the emperor and she is presently languishing in jail. Her only surviving son (by her forced marriage to *Ras* Desta when she was eleven) was executed by the Ethiopian military government in November 1974, two months after Haile Selassie was removed from power.

Haile Selassie's second son, and favorite child, Prince Makonnen, the Duke of Harar, died in an automobile accident in 1957 under unknown circumstances. Given his grandfather's name and title to the family properties in Harar, he clearly overshadowed his older brother the crown prince,

whose title was that of governor of the poorer and less important province of Wello. Haile Selassie obviously bestowed
titles and gifts upon Makonnen in order to prepare him for the
throne even though he was officially second in line. His sud-
den death caused Haile Selassie extensive grief. Upon his
death the emperor recalled his affection for the Duke of Harar.

> We loved our son Makonnen in two ways: In the first, because he is
> our son. Thus our sorrow under the shadow of his death is that of the
> heavy-laden heart of a parent at the loss of a child. Secondly, he was
> always beside us offering us essential aid and service. When we were
> in exile he was Our source of comfort. We brought him up by feeding
> him with a nursing bottle, while his mother gave him her breast. We
> had hoped that we might precede him.[2]

Prince Sahle Selassie, the youngest son, who was governor
of Gamu Goffa Province, had little interest in politics. He died
in 1962, the year of Empress Menen's death. After 1962 only
Asfa Wossen and Princess Tenegne Work remained alive.

The life of Asfa Wossen has not been a joyful one. Rumored
to be the son of former Emperor Lij Yasu, he was pressured by
Haile Selassie to marry *Ras* Seyoum's daughter in 1932 as a
political move to secure the emperor's position. Asfa Wossen
was sixteen at the time and did not wish to marry. A few years
later, he divorced this wife and remarried. Having quarrelled
violently with his father, Haile Selassie, in 1935, he was essentially exiled to Wello and resided in the city of Dessie. After
the invasion by Italy in 1935, Asfa Wossen, as governor, had
difficulty securing the allegiance of his subjects in the province because of a lingering loyalty among the residing Galla to
Lij Yasu, who had, unbeknownst to them, died three years
earlier.[3] Haile Selassie never trusted his son after the Wello
incident and when the emperor fled into exile, he brought him
along, not out of love but because Haile Selassie feared leaving him in Ethiopia where he might cause trouble. There is
absolutely no documentation to suggest that Asfa Wossen was
sired by Lij Yasu or that he would have collaborated with
Italy, but the strains between father and son were so severe
that Haile Selassie strongly believed in the latter possibility.
After the restoration Haile Selassie moved his son to Addis
Ababa where he could be watched, was said to have planted
spies in his home, and often purposely slighted him in public.

Although the prince retained the governorship of Wello, was a member of the crown council, and was first in line to the throne, he was relegated by Haile Selassie to a position of scorn.

The status of Asfa Wossen plummeted in 1960 when he was indirectly implicated in the abortive coup of that year. The revolt of December 13–14 began while the emperor was abroad on a state visit to Brazil. The six-thousand-man Imperial Guard, which had been reared to defend the emperor, revolted against the archaic feudal system. Brig. Gen. Mengistu Neway, commander of the Imperial Body Guard, and his brother Girmame, governor of Wellamo subprovince of Sidamo Province, the leaders of the rebellion, accused Haile Selassie of moving too slowly in his attempts to modernize Ethiopia. The crown prince, who later stated he was speaking at gunpoint, announced the removal of Emperor Haile Selassie. "The few selfish persons who fight merely for their own interests and for personal power, who are obstacles to progress and who, like a cancer, impede the nation's development are now replaced."[4] The crown prince was named emperor, while *Ras* Imru, whose claim that he was forced into supporting the coup was later accepted by Haile Selassie, was named prime minister of a rebel government that pledged a radical socialist and nationalist program under a constitutional monarchy.

Army troops refused to go along with the coup, and commanded by Gen. Merid Mengesha and Maj. Gen. Kebede Gebre, they successfully attacked the rebel positions December 15. The following day Haile Selassie returned to Ethiopia from Brazil where he was greeted by Crown Prince Asfa Wossen, who proclaimed his loyalty and total obedience to his father. Before the coup was completely crushed, a number of traditional patriarchs were assassinated by the rebels, which gave credence to the assumption that their radical program as a whole would have been carried out violently. Among those killed were: *Ras* Abebe Arega, minister of defense, Makonnen Habte-Wold, minister of commerce and advisor to the emperor, *Ras* Seyoum, governor-general of Tigre, and Tadessa Negash, minister of state in the justice ministry. Ironically, this was later seen by the emperor as beneficial as many of the old nobility who had opposed programs of modernization were now gone.

For the moment, however, Haile Selassie, who had come exceedingly close to losing all power and all control, struck fast and hard at the coup leaders. Mengistu was hanged, his brother reportedly committed suicide. The emperor, who normally did not have his opponents killed, clearly saw the radical nature of the Neway program and the threat of it to his position. The recollection of figures from the past reverberated inside him and the violence of his punishment represented the violence felt against those figures who had previously tried to rob him of power. This was the closest Haile Selassie had come to losing power since the restoration, and the security that he had attained since then disappeared. He was not calm and he did not wish to portray himself as a forgiving monarch. His imperial position had been threatened along with his emotional security. The Neways could have been Empress Taitu or Empress Zauditu, but more likely they represented his father who had abandoned him in death, leaving him helpless among alien forces. This of course was extraordinarily complicated by the role of Asfa Wossen. Though he publicly excused the crown prince, Haile Selassie must have identified his son with Lij Yasu and his own father, *Ras* Makonnen, all of them having acted to leave him helpless and anxious, disallowing him power over his own affairs.

Because of the complex nature of the love/hate relationship between Haile Selassie and his father, his emotional hate was tempered by an intellectual understanding of why his father could not bestow upon him the love he so wanted. Haile Selassie may also have understood what drove his son to participate, in whatever manner, in this action—his desire for revenge and to finally achieve power after waiting all these years. Since his only son was the heir to the throne, executing him would have caused difficulties in the succession, since a grandson would have had to take his place. Thus a combination of personal feelings, emotional factors, and political necessity caused him to excuse his son, and also his cousin *Ras* Imru.

Clearly, however, the emperor must have felt completely abandoned, just as he did when his father, mother, and Emperor Menelik II died. Many of his children were already dead, and now his only surviving son, and the cousin he grew up with, had caused him to question their allegiance towards him. He had now been abandoned by almost all members of his family.

Retribution against all participants in the coup who were not members of the emperor's personal family was severe. According to Greenfield, who has written the foremost analysis of the coup, 475 members of the Imperial Guard were killed in the counterattack, and 3100 were arrested, while students and all governmental and landed officials had to troop to the palace swearing total allegiance to the emperor.[5] A number of the participants were hanged, banished, or committed suicide. The emperor must have been furious with Asfa Wossen even though no evidence was ever found indicating his willingness to participate in the coup. But the history of the volatile relationship with his son and the uncertainty of his birth left Haile Selassie convinced of Asfa Wossen's guilt. Because of a lack of proof, and the complex projection of feelings he had for his own father, Haile Selassie permitted Asfa Wossen to remain free even though he had attempted, so the emperor believed, the greatest crime possible. He had tried to amputate the emperor's power, leaving him helpless and at the mercy of past anxieties. Full trust was never displayed by the emperor to his son.

After the abortive coup the crown prince was regularly in the emperor's company. Often when he traveled abroad he took his son along so as to prevent any further plundering from again taking place. Usually wherever the emperor went in Ethiopia, he was accompanied by his son, who more often than not sat quietly at his father's side, rarely speaking, and playing no role in whatever activity may have been occurring. More and more the emperor surrounded himself with his grandchildren who could often be seen romping around near him at official public gatherings. Haile Selassie, with his own children dead or untrustworthy (with the exception of Princess Tenegne Work), appeared to get joy and fulfillment from having these youngsters nearby. Often the emperor was seen being driven through the streets of Addis Ababa in one of his expensive cars with his poodle and one or another of his small grandchildren seated next to him in the back seat. He spent more time with his daughter who became, towards the end of his life, his closest advisor and friend. Asfa Wossen, who was forty-four in 1960, was left in the shadows of the family awaiting the death of his father who showed no sign of retiring and continued to be in the best of health. A heartbeat away from the monarchy, he remained as politically impotent as most vice presidents of the United States have been. The position of emperor eluded him forever and it was no accident that Haile Selassie refused to leave the throne and permit his son to rule. Needing to maintain absolute control over himself and his subjects and not wanting to allow any other to call the shots for him, Haile Selassie must have felt that the crown prince was one of the last people he wanted to see on the throne. He had not trusted his son since at least 1935, and handing power over to him would have been emotionally impossible, and politically ridiculous. One does not willingly hand power over to a potential threat. This was particularly so with Haile Selassie, who found it so emotionally necessary to control everyone. Haile Selassie would not have willingly handed power over to anyone. He never did.

The crown prince was usually reticent in public, fearful of even giving the appearance of upstaging his father. He was intent on soothing Haile Selassie's anger towards him and as a result he rarely gave interviews and was firm in remaining unassuming and in the background. In August 1967 however he invited a number of scholars to his home in Addis Ababa where over cocktails he answered a series of questions regarding his hopes and goals for Ethiopia.

Sitting on the couch in the dining room, next to his wife, Asfa Wossen was far less demanding of his retainers and servants than most persons in the imperial aristocracy. He was reserved and quite relaxed and appeared to enjoy pondering his future role as emperor. He maintained that he would do what he could to limit some of the abuses of the land system that then existed in Ethiopia so as to reduce the "amount of labor expected of farmers."[6] He did not expect that the emperor, his father Haile Selassie, would soon relinquish the throne, and he said that he did not want his father to do so. He was happy with the way things were because Haile Selassie had done extraordinary things for the country. Yes, he said, he thought about what he would like to do if and when he became emperor, but other than easing the lot of farmers, he expected he would continue the same policies as his father. He did not feel as if he were waiting for something to happen to his father, and he enjoyed the ceremonial duties that his father assigned to him. While he spoke, his children were easily and happily playing in the room and Asfa Wossen obviously enjoyed spending much time with them. There appeared to exist a close relationship between the crown prince, his wife, and their children. For about two hours he patiently answered questions, although little more of importance was said.

Not much more than this could really have been expected from the conversation with this group of Fulbright-Hays scholars. The crown prince had to be exceedingly careful in his responses. Most interesting however is that he seemed very aware of the abuse of feudalism although he sheltered his answers in benignity. He praised his father consistently, even in this area, but it was clear that he would act differently, though he never said how. In some ways he was criticizing his father within the aura of heavy praise. That however was the only contradiction in the conversation, as he generally served as adulator for Haile Selassie.

One came away from the palace feeling that buried within this adulation was an independent man, who in fact had thought a great deal about what he would do should he ever become emperor. He never clarified his goals or desires but it was clear that he had them. Although Asfa Wossen was a member of the ruling class of Ethiopia, in his person he exuded a strength, a gentleness and calmness, and an intelligence that belied the persistent and widespread rumors that he was merely a lackey to his father. There was absolutely no question in my mind that he would have tried to be a more liberal ruler than his father, and certainly he was far more intelligent and politically astute than the general Ethiopian public seemed to give him credit for. But Asfa Wossen never did attain the throne, as his father remained intent on holding on to it until the last possible moment. He apparently never forgave his son all the sins that he attributed to him, and Haile

Selassie could never overcome his need to absolutely control
the universe around him. According to Gilkes, "Haile Selassie
. . . weakened [the imperial system] very seriously by his
failure to associate the Crown Prince or any other alternative
with himself. . . . This inevitably leads to the conclusion that
he had given relatively little thought for the future of Ethiopia
after his demise. . . . his main preoccupation has been his
own survival as Emperor."[7]

Haile Selassie obviously gave little support to any of his
children. Even his favorite, Prince Makonnen, was known as a
playboy who lived for the earthy kicks of life; Haile Selassie
was hardly able to control his excesses. Two of his three
daughters died very early while his third, Tenegne Work, only
attained a close relationship when no one else was left. Asfa
Wossen was always treated by his father as a child who could
not handle responsibility. Politically impotent, the crown
prince was left to languish in semiobscurity, and never received
any love or attention from Haile Selassie. The emperor abandoned his own children in much the same way he himself was
abandoned by his own father after 1894 when his mother,
Wayzaro Yashimabet, suddenly died. Rather than compensate
through his children for the deprivation he suffered, Haile
Selassie imposed upon them the same loss and the same anxiety. This was particularly so in the case of his eldest, Asfa
Wossen, who bore the brunt of Haile Selassie's lack of care
and protection. It seems very likely that Asfa Wossen reacted
by trying to remove his father from power in 1960. It would
have been a perfectly normal reaction to the abuse Haile
Selassie heaped upon him. Haile Selassie's fury at his own
father, *Ras* Makonnen, was shifted to the crown prince. In 1935
and again in 1960 when the emperor was in danger of losing
his power he lashed out at his son who unfortunately was seen
as the image of *Ras* Makonnen. Haile Selassie could not reach
his father; in 1935 he could not attack Mussolini; in 1960 he
was very nearly removed from power—in most of these in-
stances Haile Selassie reacted against his eldest son who
clearly had become the representation of *Ras* Makonnen and
all the others who had left Tafari Makonnen alone, helpless,
and furious.

Haile Selassie may have been an emperor of long standing,

and an international figure of some repute, but he was clearly a failure as a father. His anger and anxiety were such that he could not really control this aspect of his life.

When Haile Selassie was forcibly removed from power in 1974, Asfa Wossen was in Switzerland recuperating from a severe stroke. Having borne the brunt of his father's anger, he now ironically came down with exactly the same physical ailment that had struck another who had let Haile Selassie down—Menelik II. After they took power, the leaders of the new military junta jailed most surviving members of the royal family. Although some grandchildren eventually escaped to the United States, Tenegne Work and her daughter were placed in Akaki Prison in the capital, and Princess Morshe, the eldest daughter of the crown prince, died in the same prison in January 1977 after a stomach operation. Tenegne Work's son Eskunder Desta was executed in 1974.

The sons and daughters and the grandchildren of Haile Selassie were unable to fend for themselves, and only those members of the family fortunate enough to be out of the country at the time of the 1974 coup escaped the violence directed at the Haile Selassie clan. The emperor was unable to protect his family when he was out of power, but he was unwilling to give them emotional support and love when he held power. Although little is known about Empress Menen's role in the family, it is fairly certain that Haile Selassie paid very little attention to his paternal role and instead used some of his children as foils for his own tangled relationship with his parents. In trying to work through his emotional problems via his children Haile Selassie failed at being a decent and loving father.

But he had been at his cruelest towards Asfa Wossen. It is more than likely that the emperor did not simply dismiss the rumors about his son's birth, and this only served to aggravate his anger towards the crown prince in 1935 and 1960. As the eldest son, he also served as Haile Selassie's image of *Ras* Makonnen and Lij Yasu, individuals the emperor detested because of the negative role they played in his life. Asfa Wossen's link to both sealed his fate.

The emperor's dislike of women, particularly his mother, Empress Taitu, and Empress Zauditu, was indirectly taken out on his wife and daughters. As stated earlier Haile Selassie's forced marriage to Empress Menen prevented any real emotion between the two and as a result the empress could not exert any influence upon the emperor in his role as father. She periodically supported Asfa Wossen in his disputes with Haile Selassie but to no avail. Her influence was limited. Two daughters, Zanabe Work and Tenegne Work, were themselves forced into political marriages by Haile Selassie. When Zanabe Work and Princess Tsahay died, there were no words of compassion for them in the emperor's *Selected Speeches*;[8] only for the Duke of Harar. There was clearly little feeling between Haile Selassie and his daughters, whom he used merely to serve his own selfish purposes.

By taking out his aggression on his children Haile Selassie could not have been a worse father. He was cruel, unkind, ungenerous, and merciless. He destroyed his own family unit.

12. The Whirlwind of Rebellion

In 1967 Haile Selassie became caught up in the vortex of a controversy that clarified once and for all just how potent the forces of tradition were. At the same time the events surrounding the recurring violence focused attention on the sterility of the emperor's power in engaging traditional and provincial forces that opposed his policies. The representatives of modernization and development were swept aside and lost whatever influence upon Haile Selassie they had previously attained. But perhaps the most important historical point to emerge from the explosion that erupted in 1967 is that along with the crumbling of the emperor's authority, his position on the throne was becoming more and more untenable. Following close on the heels of the abortive 1960 coup, the 1967 rebellion of the traditional forces signified the evolving erosion of Haile Selassie's power. After 1967 almost all groups recognized the powerlessness of the emperor and the temporizing position he was caught up in, being squeezed by two implacable foes—the representatives of tradition and modernization. Although few knew it at the time, history had moved against Haile Selassie and had placed him in mortal political danger. In 1967 and 1968 the absolute power of Haile Selassie was shown to be an illusion and its chimerical status became obvious to all the major contending forces in Ethiopia. Together, 1960 and 1967–68 represented the beginning of the end for Haile Selassie. His overthrow in 1974 only closed the circle begun in 1960.

The stage for the battle of 1967–68 was Haile Selassie's

income tax reform program—a far-reaching attempt by the
emperor to restrict the power of the feudal/traditional groups
that had for centuries exerted a virtually controlling influence
on the politics and economy of Ethiopia. Haile Selassie came
down hard on the side of the modernizers, i.e., on the side of
his father, *Ras* Makonnen.

A draft proclamation to amend the previous income tax laws
was made public by the ministry of finance in 1966 and had
the support of the emperor. Schedule D of draft Proclamation
No. 255 called for an agricultural income tax system that
would tax income derived from the harvest. Since no tax on
produce had ever been implemented in the past, no exemptions based on customary or traditional rules of behavior could
be claimed. This tax proposal was anything but innocent and
was fiercely opposed by all feudal and traditional forces in the
country.

Although Proclamation No. 255 also called for an increased
income tax, a tax on income from rental of land, and an increase in the business tax, Schedule D was the economic and
political centerpiece of the proposed bill.

Calling for a "tax . . . on taxable income which shall be
deemed by the gross income derived from the harvest . . . [to
be paid by persons exploiting the land] owners or tenants as
the case may be,"[1] Schedule D struck at the heart of
feudalism. The draft also called for the eventual and gradual
abolition of the tithe. Since this tax had always been shifted
upon the tenants by the landlords, this innovation was an
attempt to ease the burden of tenant farmers. The difference
between measured and unmeasured land, which through a
lack of measurement had always been utilized by landlords to
reduce their taxes, became irrelevant through the tax on produce. Unutilized land was also to be taxed, which was an
endeavor by the emperor to force the cultivation of idle lands.
According to *The Ethiopian Herald,* Schedule D was an attempt to "end the classical system of privileged exemptions."[2]
The categories of fertile, semifertile, and poor lands would
lose their importance and landowners would no longer be able
to claim successfully that fertile land was poor land because
their produce would show otherwise.

Schedule D then was more than a tax proposal. It was a

political arrow aimed at the heart of feudalism. The Ethiopian Orthodox Church was not excluded from the bill and as a result the Church felt as threatened as did the feudal barons. Taxing produce rather than land functionally meant the end of traditional and longstanding tax exemptions and private measures of taxation, but more than that it implied the eventual overthrow of the feudal structure. For feudalism in Ethiopia was based on ownership of land through which peasants were mercilessly privately taxed and exploited to the economic benefit of landlords; it required that Ethiopia remain essentially a nonindustrial state and it defined the Church and landlords as having as much authority as the central government. Through this bill, Haile Selassie tried to develop the powers of the state to the political and economic disadvantage of the traditional powers. It would strip from ownership of land its political ramifications, reduce the authority of landlords over their tenants, and force the Church and landlords to adhere to the tenets of the central government. Needless to say, this draft bill was fought tenaciously by the representatives of feudalism and provincialism.

Schedule D had been initiated in 1966 by Haile Selassie through his minister of finance, Yilma Deressa. Burdened by the pressures placed upon him in 1960 by the forces of modernization, the emperor tried to push quickly for reforms. Yilma Deressa, who had been close to the emperor since the restoration in 1941, was in favor of change, and being totally loyal to the emperor, was selected via his official position for the arduous task of constructing the bill and seeing it through parliament.

Yilma Deressa, after the abortive coup in 1960, was able to put through measures in his own department that would allow him to combat the conservatism so rampant in Ethiopia. In the 1960s a number of younger officials in the ministry were sent to the United States for advanced training in finance. Among them was Eshetu Habtegiorgis, a man who was destined to play a formidable but futile role in the process of obtaining parliamentary passage of the draft proclamation.[3] Yilma Deressa, Eshetu Habtegiorgis, the director of the ministry's legal department, Bulcha Demeksa and Tefferi Lemma, the two vice-ministers, and two European tax advisors, Oscar A.

Spencer and Ernest Zaremba, fashioned the bill and prepared
its language.

Before the bill went to parliament the council of ministers
and the crown council approved it. With the emperor behind
the bill, the traditional crown council had little choice but
ratification since its relationship to the emperor was on a
personal level. It could not utilize nonpersonal bureaucratic
procedures to destroy the bill. By the end of 1966 the bill was
presented to the chamber of deputies for ratification, and upon
passage would be sent to the senate.[4] Eshetu was selected by
Yilma Deressa to be the official lobbyist of the ministry of
finance in parliament.

In February 1967 the chamber of deputies took the bill
under consideration. Haile Selassie, using the ministry of
finance as an instrument, attempted to stem the power of the
traditional forces in the country. "In this instance he both
alienated the forces of tradition and . . . forever lost control
over the forces of modernization. The forces of tradition and
modernization both increased their power in 1967/1968 while
Haile Selassie lost power to both."[5]

Prime Minister Aklilu Habte Wold and Yilma Deressa presented the draft Proclamation to the chamber of deputies,
arguing for its quick approval. But the chamber had other
ideas and its actions in this case set a precedent. For the first
time since its institution in 1931, parliament disassembled and
completely reassembled a government bill. The chamber of
deputies and the senate established a role in policy-making
that neither house had taken previously, and temporarily altered the process of decision-making in Ethiopia. Parliament
became a major force attempting to stem the tide of modernization. Since all members were property owners and most
were feudal lords in their own right, they felt personally and
politically threatened by the bill.

The chamber of deputies zeroed in on the four parts of
Schedule D: (1) the method of assessment, (2) the tax on
unutilized land, (3) the tithe, and (4) the rate of taxation.[6] In the
first instance parliament succeeded in placing the assessment
process in the hands of local/provincial landed elites and taking it out of the hands of the national government. The tax on
unused land was vetoed. Rather than abolishing the tithe after

a period of time when tax from the new proclamation was substantial enough so that the government could carry on without it, parliament eliminated it immediately. In point of fact this allowed the landlords to continue collecting the tithe from tenant farmers and retaining it for themselves. The rate of taxation was passed in its original form as it was purposely regressive in an attempt to expand the number of taxed persons. All in all the chamber of deputies voted to nullify the tax insofar as feudal powers were concerned, but passed those measures that applied to the peasants. The senate voted in exactly the same way.

As a result of its actions in 1967, parliament not only established a major role for itself in decision-making but it became a major force representing tradition. Since the Church made it clear that it would not allow the new tax law, however it emerged from parliament, to be applied to it, both houses of parliament felt secure that the emperor would have to go along with their proposals. Once again Haile Selassie was shown the vitality of tradition in Ethiopia and was powerless to do anything about it. In 1960 he was pushed by modern elements, and now he was being shoved around by traditional groups. He had no intention of putting himself on the line by publicly coming out in strong support of the bill as never did he allow himself to be too closely associated with defeat. Someone else would have to pay. His unwillingness to do more than make his views known and to directly pressure parliament allowed the latter to believe it could get away with altering the bill to suit its own purposes. Parliament was correct. As in 1944, Haile Selassie backed down in the face of overwhelming unity among feudal authorities.

Nonetheless, Proclamation No. 255 of 1967 was passed by parliament November 23, 1967, in its altered form, and the ministry of finance had every intention of applying it wherever possible. Landlords and the Church remained untouched by it insofar as they could control assessment committees, but the ministry of finance and the ministry of land reform and administration tried to implement the law as best they could. Both ministries were now in the position of being the central structures representing modernization within the bureaucracy and they remained firm in upholding that status. In early

1968 committees were established to measure produce for the purpose of taxation. This led to a major rebellion in the province of Gojam that generated the political dismemberment of both ministries, destroyed Proclamation No. 255 in its infancy, forced Haile Selassie to retreat from the law's application, and led to the political growth of junior officers in the military who were among those called upon by the emperor to put down the armed revolt in Gojam. The rebellion in Gojam became another plank in the political coffin of Haile Selassie.

Because of a serious manpower shortage, assessment teams could not be established in all districts. Teams would skirt some areas and avoid others completely, while many teams would depend on the word of the *chiqa shum* (chief) to inform them of the amount of harvest produced per tenant and landlord. The result was a great degree of inaccuracy, and appeal commissions were kept extraordinarily busy. Weather was also a variable and if the rains were heavy, teams avoided the area.

In Sidamo Province and in other parts of Ethiopia land remained unutilized until after the assessment was concluded, thereby allowing landowners to avoid taxation. In huge chunks of Ethiopia, tax assessors dared not approach many of the very large landowners because of their political or economic clout. The ministry of finance, having no knowledge of the amount of land owned by individual holders, and being severely hampered by a lack of trained personnel, could do little to rectify the situation.[7]

But it was in Gojam where the most volatile opposition to assessment took place.[8] Farmers reacted violently when the government sent tax assessors into the province in 1968. There were two fundamental reasons for their opposition. (1) Since the government considered payment of land tax one of the means of determining and affixing private ownership of land, the Gojamies felt, and rightfully so, that by accepting the law they would be relinquishing their communal land status and would be opening the door to the destruction of communalism. (2) The governor-general of Gojam, *Dejazmatch* Tsehai Inqu Selassie, was despised by the Gojamies because of his arbitrary and oppressive behavior towards the province. A Shoan-Amhara, the Gojam-Amhara considered him a foreigner who ruthlessly attempted to collect taxes from the Church and the farmers. A retainer of Haile Selassie, he grew up in the Imperial Palace and was more than willing to do the emperor's bidding.

When tax assessors initially entered Gojam many land-owners refused to allow them onto the land. There was little organization of this opposition, and when fighting did break out in some areas, it was spontaneous. Assessors became frightened and sought protection from the territorial army which was under the authority of the governor-general. The army moved to protect the tax assessors.

From December 1967 to April 1968 violence was only intermittent. The territorial army appeared to have control of the situation and the subprovinces of Agew Midir and Metekel caused little trouble. In May 1968, however, the situation began to deteriorate. The population of the subprovinces of Bahir Dar, Bichena, Debre Markos, Dega-Damot, and Motta, which occupy the eastern portion of Gojam, began to organize and block assessment. A group of farmers who held rights to land in Motta traveled the subprovince urging farmers to stop assessment teams from entering onto their land. Through May and June this farmer group spread its doctrine of resistance, although no permanent political structure was established to coordinate the movement. It was not difficult for the activists to convince other farmers that assessment meant the end of communalism and should be halted. Using rifles acquired during the Italian occupation of the 1930s the Gojamies fought off the assessment teams and the territorial army.

The governor-general sent more troops into the area and bloodshed followed. Many *chiqa shums* were killed as were some farmers and members of the territorial army. The number of farmers who joined the farmer group reached into the hundreds, and at this point the movement expanded south to the neighboring subprovince of Bichena. Tsehai responded by ordering part of the territorial army into Bichena and insisting that tax assessors proceed with their job. By early July, Motta and Bichena were in a virtual state of revolt. Neither the emperor, the finance ministry, nor the defense ministry acted, and the violence continued unchecked.

Following its success in Motta and Bichena, the farmer

group, which now numbered three to four thousand members, moved west into Dega-Damot, which became the toughest center of resistance. Clashes erupted between the territorial army and farmers and many were killed and wounded. For all practical purposes tax assessment in the three subprovinces was at a standstill.

The farmer group then moved to challenge the emperor directly. Thousands of farmers flocked into Debre Markos, the provincial capital, which had now joined the revolt. The emperor was informed that if assessment were not immediately halted, the Blue Nile Bridge, which connects Beghemdir Province with Gojam, would be blown up. The farmer group also demanded the removal of Governor Tsehai. The entire province was in direct revolt against the emperor and the tax law.

In mid-July 1968 Haile Selassie through the defense ministry ordered some nine hundred troops of the national government into Gojam. Most of them were stationed in Motta, Debre Markos, and near the Blue Nile Bridge. The Ethiopian Air Force was used to bomb villages in Gojam that quartered the resistance fighters. But the turmoil continued, and two weeks later tax assessment was halted; in May 1969 the emperor cancelled all arrears of taxation in Gojam for the previous nineteen years.

The Ethiopian Herald reported on August 3, 1968, that Tsehai Inqu Selassie had been demoted to deputy governor-general of Kaffa Province[9], while on February 8, 1969, Yilma Deressa was fired from the finance ministry and was appointed minister of commerce, industry, and tourism. No taxation of any kind was imposed on Gojam after 1967 as the province remained free from the authority of the national government and Haile Selassie.

Clearly, the ministry of finance and the ministry of land reform and administration were in favor of destroying communalism in Gojam and pressured Haile Selassie into standing up to the province. The Gojam-Amhara, who are looked down upon by the Shoan-Amhara, were hardly represented in the central government, and therefore had little direct influence upon the emperor. In alliance with the emperor the two ministries opposed negotiations as they were clearly aware that in 1944 the Gojamies succeeded in having themselves excluded from the 1942 land tax proclamation. But closing the channels of political communication, and resorting to high levels of armed force, alienated the Gojamies further from the regime, and caused them to act more violently than they would have had there been negotiations. Haile Selassie, however, never negotiated his position of authority particularly when directly challenged. The failure to negotiate only served to increase the level of violence. The Gojamies had absolutely nothing to lose, for by successfully standing up to the government they would be able to maintain their communal system of land tenure. Thus they fought bravely and fiercely and the army remained powerless to stop the rebellion. Only total capitulation to the demands of Gojam enabled the emperor to stop the growing rebellion to his authority. Gojam had thoroughly defeated the powers of Addis Ababa.

Parliament's opposition to Haile Selassie and the rebellion of Gojam pointed out how rapidly feudal and provincial forces would unify to stem the tide of change. The emperor's unwillingness to force the issue showed how acutely aware he was of the powers of tradition, even though he emotionally stood together with the forces of modernization. What was of utmost importance to him was the preservation of his power and his throne even if the office of emperor was ineffective throughout Ethiopia. Political authority was of far less importance than the maintenance of power and position. As usual Haile Selassie took some major steps forward, and when the traditional opposition was aroused he quickly backtracked to a position even more conservative than the one he had started with. Not only did Gojam remain untaxed but almost twenty years of previously uncollected taxes were rescinded.

In large part the emperor's role in this issue symbolized the competing influences pressuring him. A supporter of reform, he was still firmly entrenched in the class of Shoan aristocrats who had ruled Ethiopia with a feudal whip for centuries. He could not easily challenge the Amharic class which he was so firmly embedded in. At the same time he was scared to death of losing his throne and being again helpless and without the political levers that gave him such control over others on a personal, if not political, level.

Haile Selassie made the strongest stand of his career over the issue of Proclamation No. 255 of 1967, but the position taken was neither very strong nor very dogmatic. He refused to associate himself with the draft bill, other than giving it his blessing and asking house members to support it. He would not place his prestige on the line for it, nor would he battle Gojam to the death over it. Neither was as important as remaining on the throne, and to do that it was clear in 1967 that he still needed the support of the Church and of the landlords. He would not cut off his head for the sake of Ethiopia. In this way he was a true supporter of feudalism even if the appearance was otherwise. He was not a true believer in reform, only a tentative one. He wanted reform but he needed tradition to stay in power. Thus he temporized, allowing modern elements to push him forward, then permitting traditional forces to shove him back. But in the process, unbeknownst to him, he lost the support of both groups, and isolated himself politically. In fact this was careless politics as it served to easily permit him to be overthrown only a few years later. But at this time it fit the pattern of his entire political history. It was his way of maintaining power and not permitting any other person or group from obtaining enough power to challenge his position.

There could not be reform or progress in Ethiopia if Haile Selassie's position would, in his view, be weakened. Thus, there could be no reform at all because his position would be weakened, perhaps destroyed, by traditional powers. In 1967–1968 the forces of modernization, particularly in the military, came to recognize once and for all that they could not depend on the emperor to sponsor real change. He would not ever complete what he had started. They saw sharply how much control traditional representatives had over him and how quickly he was prepared to do their bidding. I would argue that in the long run this political recognition by the junior officers in the military establishment was the ultimate disaster for Haile Selassie in 1967–68. These officers saw, particularly in Gojam, how quickly Haile Selassie would retreat and how impotent he really was in bringing about political and economic reforms.

In parliament and in Gojam Haile Selassie had boxed himself into a corner and very soon forces of change would block any exit from that corner. In 1967–68 Haile Selassie made one final lunge at reform. It was a spectacular one that led to a spectacular and unredeemable failure. Soon Haile Selassie would pay the price of all his abortive attacks on tradition.

Never again would Haile Selassie push hard for reform and in the years 1969–1974, while Haile Selassie traveled abroad, involved himself with the affairs of Africa, and remained content to exercise very little domestic authority, segments of the Ethiopian military, disgusted with Haile Selassie's inaction, would prepare for the final denouement in the life of the Lion of Judah.

13. Revolution and the Fall from Power

Ethiopia's revolution began as just another army mutiny—the kind of "local difficulty" which Emperor Haile Selassie has been accustomed to handling from the time he was a stripling warrior at the Court of Menelik. . . . But, on this occasion, he behaved uncharacteristically: instead of sending a strong army unit down to Negelle . . . to deal with the army mutineers, he chose appeasement. It was a fateful error.[1]

For the first time in his long reign Haile Selassie could not effectively strike at his opponents and it cost him his throne. It began in February 1974. In the wake of civil disturbances reflecting public concern over unemployment, increasing prices, soaring inflation, and a spreading famine which took the lives of hundreds of thousands of people in 1973–74,[2] dissident military forces took over a number of Ethiopian cities and surrounded all public buildings in the capital city of Addis Ababa. Calling for military pay raises, land reform programs, and the dismissal of the cabinet, junior officers who organized the revolt forced Haile Selassie to submit to all their demands by March. During March and April, strikes—an unheard-of phenomenon in Ethiopia—took place throughout the country. With the support of the military rebels, higher wages that were demanded by the strikers were granted by the emperor.

The government headed by Aklilu Habte Wold was dismissed by the emperor and replaced by one headed by Endalkachew Makonnen, another member of the Ethiopian aristocracy. The rebel leaders were not appeased by the new government which refused to implement the land reform measures demanded by them. Removal of additional authorities was called for and in turn the emperor fired the lord mayor of Addis Ababa, the deputy military chief of staff, and a number of provincial governors-general. Haile Selassie appeared unable to quell the military and civilian upheavals that exploded upon him that year. On March 5 and April 14, however, he made two major moves in an effort to halt the growing disorders and threats to his imperial authority. On March 5 he called for a thirty-member constitutional convention to bring about political reforms and an alteration of the feudal economic structure. On April 14 Haile Selassie finally named a successor to the throne—his twenty-one-year-old grandson, Prince Zara Yacob, son of the invalid Crown Prince Asfa Wossen. Given the history of Haile Selassie's stormy relationship with Asfa Wossen the crown prince's removal from the line of succession was to be expected and the excuse used by the emperor was his son's illness. Prince Zara Yacob, a college student in England, refused the emperor's request that he return to Ethiopia. His presence in Ethiopia was, at this time, unnecessary. The belatedness and irony of this move is that for years Haile Selassie had ignored "the advice of virtually all his closest advisors, including the chairman of the Crown Council, *Ras* Asrate Kassa, and his Prime Minister, Aklilu Habte Wold, who had been urging on him for at least three years that he should make way on his 80th birthday . . . for an orderly succession through his son, the Crown Prince, Asfa Wossen, and his grandson, Prince Zara Yacob . . . [in order to] defend the old Shoan supremacy. . . ."[3]

The moves fell far short of the junior officers' expectations[3] and unsatisfied with the creeping pace of events, they ordered officials of the former government of Aklilu Habte Wold arrested. Among those jailed in June were some of the scions of the Shoan-Amhara establishment: *Ras* Kassa, Yilma Deressa, a former minister of finance, Minassie Haile, a former minister of foreign affairs. The military dissidents again demanded of the emperor that political and social reforms proceed rapidly.

Endalkachew Makonnen, the prime minister, a wealthy landowner and a firm believer in the feudal system, tried to appease the military leaders of the movement via the rhetoric of change but proceeded at a snail's pace to implement any reforms, and did what he could to hamper the movement of the constitutional convention. On July 22, angered by his indecision and inability to act progressively, the rebel Military Coordinating Committee placed Endalkachew Makonnen under arrest and forced the emperor to appoint as prime minister Michael Imru, a liberal member of the Shoan aristocracy. The Committee continued to arrest public leaders whom it blamed for the mass starvation that had occurred during the drought, and for the continued maintenance of feudalism. By September 1974 more than two hundred and fifty Ethiopian leaders were imprisoned in the basement of the Grand Palace, where the emperor had his office. Others were put in Akaki prison in the center of Addis Ababa where many of the emperor's family were also incarcerated. All the emperor's associates and his palace retainers were arrested by this time.

In early August, Michael Imru announced that a draft constitution had been completed. The draft would make the emperor a constitutional monarch, severely limit his powers, and give increased power, including the right to select a prime minister, to the elected parliament. But the military junta, under the leadership of Lt. Col. Mengistu Haile Mariam, who was a Shankella, a group detested by the Amhara, Lt. Gen. Aman Michael Andom, an Eritrean who as a young boy returned with the emperor to Ethiopia from the Sudan where his family had been in exile during the Italian occupation, and Brig. Gen. Teferi Banti, a Shoan who served for a time as military attache in Washington, D.C., were not impressed. Furious that Haile Selassie seemed to be using constitutional structures to bury the demands of the military in a bureaucratic pit, the junta deposed Haile Selassie September 12, 1974, and had him arrested.

Two months later fifty-nine major officials and some of the key scions of the imperial aristocracy were executed in batches of ten. Among those murdered were Aklilu Habte Wold and Endalkachew Makonnen, the two former prime ministers, *Ras* Kassa, president of the crown council, Mesfin Sileshi, the former governor of Shoa Province, Abeje Debaki, a supreme court judge, Blatta Admassu Retta, the private treasurer of Haile Selassie, and Haile Selassie's grandson Eskunder Desta, a former commander of the Navy.[4] All were accused of corruption, embezzlement of funds, and maladministration.

Lt. Col. Mengistu Haile Mariam, a self-proclaimed Marxist who later emerged as the real power behind the military junta, found no need to apologize for the executions and murders of literally thousands of his opponents that followed the overthrow of the emperor. In 1978 he maintained that "our struggle is a calculated and scientific attempt to neutralize the power of the reactionary forces. . . . The revolution has an obligation to those who have been deprived and oppressed for centuries. Its goal is to build a socialist society in which justice, freedom, equality . . . prevail."[5]

Since 1960, when the abortive coup against Haile Selassie had occurred, the Ethiopian military had recognized its political power. To keep the armed forces in line, pay raises were granted by the emperor in 1961; these had previously been rejected by the emperor as an unnecessary financial burden. In 1965, in a further effort to develop the support of the military, serving members of the armed forces were granted tax-free title to forty hectares of land each. Using traditional sources of patronage, Haile Selassie had tried to cohere a modern military to an archaic and traditional Ethiopia. But it had just the opposite effect during a time that the political consciousness of higher-echelon junior officers was increasing as the realization struck them that in 1960 the armed forces had been the only force able to prevent the overthrow of Haile Selassie. With new political awareness, political demands upon the emperor were generated. The military was no longer apolitical and was not prepared to do the emperor's bidding unless he accepted its demands. Haile Selassie, by advancing financial benefits to the military, assumed it could be bought off so that it would not question a regime which after 1960 was kept in power via its guns. The techniques honed and developed through the years to garner the allegiance of the myriad political sectors of Ethiopia no longer operated with precision. For Haile Selassie, in constructing a military to support him in his attempt to modernize the country, had created a political force that tried to coerce the emperor into moving more quickly than he was willing to. After 1960 his authority over the military declined as it clearly saw that the political legitimacy of Haile Selassie's regime was nonexistent.

Independent political consciousness was also developed within the military leadership in both the Eritrean conflict and the 1967–68 Gojam rebellion. With half the army stationed in Eritrea, opposing the secessionist Eritrean liberation armies, and with some one thousand troops utilized to halt the Gojam rebellion, the military became starkly aware that it was not only defending the political structure but the entire feudal fabric of Ethiopia. In the ensuing years its political education was reinforced by the spate of books that appeared and precisely analyzed the Ethiopian feudal structure.[6]

Gojam, a rebellion the emperor could not cope with, took on political overtones above its apparent meaning. It pointed out the stunning weakness of imperial authority. Officers and junior officers became aware that the construct of the regime was dependent upon their action. If Gojam was such a threat, then the revolutionary situation posed by the ELF/EPLF in Eritrea was far more politically dangerous to the regime and its ideology than had previously been noted. The 1960 coup suggested the possibility of a student, intellectual, military, peasant front in opposition to the feudal system. This became apparent when the coup leaders contacted elements of these other groups and received verbal support for their actions. Gojam showed the weakness of the government in dealing with nonrevolutionary violence of a feudal nature. And the inability of the Haile Selassie government to stem the movement of the ever more powerful and successful liberation fighters in Eritrea showed clearly the regime's political weakness in halting revolutionary violence. Together, the 1960 abortive coup, Gojam, and Eritrea, showed the contradictions inherent in the ruling class and its inability to deal with violently articulated opposition. Compromise and negotiation were not possible when the feudal structure was called into question.

A growing number of university students have been involved in political activity since 1960. With the stymied coup as the takeoff point, many students at Haile Selassie I University have since 1967 articulated their growing anger with both Haile Selassie and the state.[7] Students pressured for land reform in 1967, 1968, and 1974, and for political reform within the university in 1968, 1969, and 1970. The latter three years students demanded an end to the growing number of Indian and United States teachers, particularly the Peace Corps volunteers, and a greater degree of Ethiopianization within the university. In this they succeeded as the Peace Corps program was drastically curtailed and the number of Indian teachers was cut. In 1972, after repeated protests by students on campus against the school-leaving exam required of high school students, government troops and police stormed the college campus in Addis Ababa and some two thousand students were arrested and expelled from school. The students too were rebelling against Haile Selassie whom they accused of moving too slowly in his reforms. Both the students and the military had moved far ahead of the emperor politically.

Though largely reformist, the students, under the regime of Haile Selassie, represented a potential link between three groups: the younger military officers who opposed the state, had the guns, and were not tied directly to the aristocracy; the urban proletariat, which became more and more outspoken in its discontent; and the peasants. Through the Ethiopian University Service (EUS) in which the third year of university was spent in the interior teaching or aiding in agricultural development, the student body had the ability to communicate its discontent to the peasant, and did so. Thus, the 1960 coup, Gojam, Eritrea, and the government violence against students were essential factors that tied together opposition to the feudal Ethiopian regime into a loose political community. The obvious weaknesses of the government had been recognized by these groups and in 1974 this loose community became firmly intertwined and, led by junior officers of the army, destroyed the government of Haile Selassie.[8]

On three crucial occasions, in 1960, in 1968–69 in Gojam, and in 1974 when Haile Selassie was finally overthrown, the emperor's authority based in the shifting sand of charisma, tradition, and feudalism, was not adequate to maintain the loyalty of significant groups within the population. His long-standing ability to reconcile competing interests within the context of reform failed, and failed largely because reform was absolutely impossible given the feudal nature of the regime. Over the long run reform meant destruction of the feudal elite and this group was intent on preserving its status and role in the system. Even in 1974 *Ras* Kassa, and prime ministers Aklilu Habte Wold and Endalkachew Makonnen lobbied strenuously to pressure the emperor into not granting the reforms demanded by the Dergue (the Military Coordinating Committee) so that the feudal society could be preserved.[9] The more radical elements in Ethiopia—junior officers and students—remained unsatisfied since their goals were impossible to achieve within the structure of authority established and represented by Haile Selassie. The evolving political awareness of the military throughout the 1960s added to their sense of power; the starvation that occurred in 1973–74 due to the horrible drought that hit Ethiopia, and the emperor's attempt to cover it up because of its negative effect on Ethiopia's image abroad, was the straw that broke the back of the camel.[10] In 1974 the armed forces moved.

In the first months of 1974 when junior officers made explicit demands and the emperor was meeting these demands, traditionals in Ethiopia fought every step of the way despite the possible consequences of a direct military takeover. Haile Selassie was caught in an impossible political bind. His authority over the military, weak since 1960, forced him to agree to its demands; this in turn weakened his authority over traditional conservative allies who themselves tried to disrupt the reform movement of the Dergue. This was the same dilemma faced by Haile Selassie in 1967–1968 when he attempted to reform the land tax system and alienated parliament and Gojam. As I said then:

> [The government in its effort] to break down tradition [has] alerted the forces representing tradition who see the threat to their political existence and have therefore prepared politically and physically to combat institutional application of modern legislation. So too however, have the forces representing modernization been alerted; forces who feel the Emperor is not moving quickly enough in bringing about change. Thus, the interests both of the traditional sector and the modernizing sector raise pressures impossible for the government to accommodate, and which are likely to be increasingly difficult to maintain within the political system now in existence.[11]

In 1974 all the contradictions came back to haunt Haile Selassie and there was no possible exit from this dilemma. Haile Selassie was overthrown and all the structures of his government, including the monarchy, were abolished.

One of the more troublesome questions to arise from the
events of 1974 is why Haile Selassie did not immediately
crack down hard on the military rebels when the rumblings of
disorder began in February? After all, throughout his reign the
emperor had always shown little mercy to those who tried to
overthrow him or tried to severely curtail his imperial authority. Those opponents that had tried to simply neutralize his
authority had been bought off with land patronage, and if
powerful enough, had been let alone if they agreed to allow
the emperor total dominance over the national political structures. But to those who were potent and direct threats to his
power, little allowance was granted and removal from position, prison, exile, or death were the results sure to follow from
such treasonous behavior.

In 1974, however, Haile Selassie opted for a policy of appeasement, contrary to all tactics theretofore practiced by him.
Although initially the junta leaders pushed for a reform program, it became quickly evident that as each demand was
granted by Haile Selassie, another was generated. Appeasement permitted the Dergue to believe that it could get whatever it wanted because acceptance of demands was seen as
weakness by the rebel forces. Under the banner of *Ethiopia
Tikdem* (Ethiopia First), the junta's junior officers, seeing that
the emperor would not act against them, moved quickly and in
June arrested a large number of senior officers who in most
cases were pillars of the Shoan establishment. Without any
superior military leadership to challenge them, the junior
officers were now assured of the loyalty of the rank and file.
The jailing of high-ranking officers prevented any alternative
military force from opposing the Dergue. In and of itself this
action was a coup d'etat as it removed any obstacle to the
Dergue's power and left it free to act as it desired. Though the
emperor was not removed from power until September, the
June arrests of civilian and military authorities doomed Haile
Selassie. Still, from February to May, Haile Selassie appeared
to have some limited freedom of maneuver by which he could
have tried to manipulate those forces opposed to the Dergue to
act in unison against it. What prevented this from taking place?

In the first place the junta's junior officers were by this time
the most politicized group in the country and were keenly

aware of what they had to do to first achieve authority and then power. They were clearly unwilling to let anything stand in their way. Secondly, the military had a monopoly on guns and the Dergue made it clear to senior officers that opposition to it might mean death. This stilled the senior echelon for an important period of time. Third, the issue of Ethiopian starvation and the emperor's willingness to tolerate Ethiopian deaths for the sake of international prestige alienated wide segments of the civil service, student body, workers, and farmers. In fact, civil servants were the one group of people who had readily supported Haile Selassie's moves for development and modernization but they were so repelled by inaction on the issue of hunger that almost as a group they supported the Dergue. Fourth, the traditional forces, as represented by the landlords, were not unified, and in the case of a coup somewhat powerless. Some pushed the emperor to forcefully quell the disturbance, while others, particularly provincial elites, were angered by Haile Selassie's continued emphasis on reform and refused to give him their support. At the same time the power of traditional forces rested in areas where the national government had little effective control and many provincial powers saw little to gain from entering the fray. They obviously felt, erroneously it turns out, that no government would be able to impinge upon their authority.

Haile Selassie throughout his reign tried to balance off traditional and modern forces, giving a little to the latter and a little more to the former. In so doing the emperor was unable to garner substantial support from either of the two sides. While the military supported him this policy sufficed to keep him in power, but when large segments of the armed forces turned against him there was no group whatsoever that was willing to support the emperor and there was certainly no group that had any independent political standing that could offset the moves of the military. The civil service was weak, as the bureaucracy was in its infancy; parliament was impotent; there was no party structure in the political system as parties had always been disallowed, and the educated elite were generally opposed to the emperor and his snail-paced efforts at reform. The major political powers were landlords, the Church, and the new political elites who served within the executive government. The landlords were divided and not militarily oriented to act in unison against this kind of opposition; the Church's power rested on tradition and influence over traditional powers such as the emperor but it held no sway over the military; and the new political elites were politically beholden to the emperor and generally had no independent sources of power. So the emperor was all alone and in large part this was his own fault. He had always refused to allow the creation of viable and organized power groups independent from himself. When the major dependent group tore itself from his grip, possessed the guns, and proceeded to act against the emperor, no countervailing source of power, other than senior military officers, was available, and since they had little authority over the rank and file, as the growing mutiny made clear, their power was stilled and Haile Selassie had to try to appease his way out of the enclosing vise.

Haile Selassie built up the position of emperor to the political disadvantage of other groups in society. Thus when he truly needed political support there was literally none to be had. The emotional insecurity always felt by the emperor had a lot to do with this as it disallowed him from dealing with groups or individuals in any capacity other than subordinating them to his own absolute control. Moving too slowly on reform to satisfy the moderns, he was seen as acting too quickly to suit the traditionals. Neither group supported him fully, and Haile Selassie was unable to obtain the political clout that would have been of immense aid to him in 1974. Although granting some aims to each group gave Haile Selassie total control over everything since both were always struggling for position, in effect the emperor was only in control of the system so long as all groups played by his rules and he played by theirs. When this changed the absolute power turned to dust and was quickly blown away. In the final analysis the so-called absolute monarch controlled very little. Ironically, the need to attain absolute control over his life and over his subjects disallowed him the real authority he so needed when challenged.

The insecurity and anxiety that Haile Selassie was so much a prisoner of, and had been since his abandonment in childhood, forced him to attain power and at the same time caused him to lose it. Attempting to compensate for the feeling of helplessness caused by the death of his parents prevented full accommodation with any group in society. Thus, no allies were there to aid the emperor when he was in the process of losing total control of Ethiopia. Appeasement therefore was the only reasonable policy Haile Selassie could entertain in 1974 because there was no alternative. There was no countervailing political authority that Haile Selassie could have conceivably called upon to stop the armed forces from taking power. But appeasement and manipulation did not succeed where it had so often in the past because this group of military officers was ideologically and politically committed to radical social change and remained unwilling to compromise in any way whatsoever. Since its accession to power the Dergue has been involved in a continuing gun battle with all opposing forces and it has exiled, imprisoned, executed, or murdered all those opponents it could lay its hands on.[12] Revolutionary violence occurs daily on the streets of Addis Ababa, where each morning bodies that litter the streets and sidewalks from nightly gun battles have to be carted away for burial. This is the kind of ideological entity that can not be bought off.

Haile Selassie had constructed a regime that in the end left him as completely helpless as he had been as a child. His life had come full circle, and he was at the end virtually alone, effectively helpless, and completely abandoned. Old, and said to be somewhat senile, it is reasonable to believe that the fear and anxiety he experienced as a youth, upon the deaths of his parents and Menelik II, were not as intense in 1974. According to those with access to him after his arrest, Haile Selassie was unwilling to go into exile even if permitted to by the Dergue, which gives some indication of the reduced level of the anxiety. "I am an old man and I've been in exile once in my life; I've no desire to become an exile again."[13]

There was no hope left. Power was lost and could not be regained. But Haile Selassie had been emperor for forty-four years, and the effective ruler of Ethiopia for fifty-eight years. He had retained for much longer than he could or should have expected the political power and control he had so longed for decades ago. Although angry at being thrown out of power so ignobly, and helpless to do anything about it, whatever despair he felt could not match that displayed prior to 1930.

Haile Selassie believed he had succeeded in establishing control over life far longer than most.

Yet, the largest contradiction of all is that in fact he was never in true control but was always seeking to attain it. Haile Selassie had failed as emperor and as a person. The entire structure of government collapsed because of Haile Selassie's unwillingness to tolerate the establishment of legal-rational structures of government that might be effective. And he never achieved the total control of his own personal universe that would allow him emotional security. *Thus his inability to achieve emotional control led to his unwillingness to reduce his power and delegate it to others, and to his refusal to permit viable national institutions from coming into existence, and this was the primary cause for the collapse of the Ethiopian social system.* His insecure emotional state led to the destruction of Ethiopia as he knew it. As a man and as an emperor he failed to achieve what was necessary for Ethiopia and for himself. And the failure to achieve his own emotional needs led to the havoc and disorder that erupted after 1974.

Haile Selassie thus serves as an excellent case study of the relationship between the personal and the political. The linkage between the two is evident and displays how the emotional makeup of the ruler can distort the rule. Haile Selassie defined the style of his politics via his emotions, allowing them to rule his politics. Because he could never quite satisfy his inner self, he left Ethiopia in ruins.

14. History Will Judge

On the afternoon of September 10, 1974, five representatives of the Military Coordinating Committee, supported by hundreds of troops, arrived at Jubilee Palace to confer with Haile Selassie. In the presence of Zewde Gabre-Selassie, the foreign minister and former mayor of Addis Ababa, who was serving as the informal liaison between the military and the emperor, Haile Selassie was asked about a reported $1 billion that the junta accused him of having stolen and banked in Switzerland. The military was demanding the return of the money to Ethiopia. The emperor denied he had taken any money, denied he had given it to his children or grandchildren, and denied he had invested it in either Ethiopia or Switzerland. With his hands waving jauntily he claimed that those who accused him of this did not understand Ethiopian history since "an emperor sits for life and has no need to take money for future exigencies. There is no money."[1] With a faint hint of a smile, he turned to the officers and said, "All I have done is take care of my family in the same way I took care of all of you."[2] This point was not lost on the officers, who, since 1960, had been pampered and patronized by the emperor in his effort to secure their allegiance to him. The officers left the palace but returned two days later to arrest Haile Selassie. The emperor was finally toppled from power.

Little is known about how the emperor spent his final year under palace arrest. The Dergue, fearing that the emperor could be used by its opponents as a rallying point, issued no information on his activities. After being moved from one palace to another, he finally died in his sleep of old age and illness August 27, 1975. He was buried quickly and secretly. Of his allies and sycophants more is known.[3] Tsehai Inqu Selassie, the former governor of Gojam, had gone into hiding until he was flushed out by the army a few days prior to Haile Selassie's removal from power. He died fighting the junta. Yilma Deressa, the former finance minister, first worked together with the junta as an advisor until he was arrested and placed in the basement jail of the palace where he still languishes. Aklilu Habte Wold and Endalkachew Makonnen, the two former prime ministers, were executed on what has come to be known as Bloody Saturday, November 23, 1974, while Michael Imru, the last prime minister of Ethiopia, has disappeared and is presumed to be in jail (for a short while prior to his disappearance he was a political advisor to the Dergue). Zewde Gabre-Selassie resigned as foreign minister in 1974 after the November executions and remained in New York City, living in exile. Asfa Wossen, the crown prince, is in exile in Geneva, Switzerland, while his sister, Princess Tenegne Work, has been festering in prison since September 11, 1974. Getachew Mekasha, a favorite of Haile Selassie, and appointed to a position in the emperor's cabinet, turned against the emperor and was selected by the junta to be ambassador to Egypt. After Bloody Saturday he was ordered to return to Ethiopia. He refused, resigned from the government and went into exile in the United States. *Ras* Kassa, president of the crown council, was also executed in November 1974. Eshetu Habtegiorgis worked for a time for the junta, and was sent to Harvard University for further study. He returned to Ethiopia in 1976. Haile Selassie's fall from power was complete as almost all the emperor's personal and political entourage were executed, jailed, or fled into exile. Only those who had at one time or another differed with the emperor, and had made their differences known, were allowed to live and to play a role, however minor, in the new government.

But few in history are either all good or all evil, and this was just as true of Haile Selassie. Certainly within Ethiopia he did little to better the human rights of his population although he periodically tried to reform the worst elements of the feudal system they were prisoners of. In this he failed largely because he was himself a representative of the oppressive ruling class and he knew that he could not survive in power unless he acceded to its demands. So throughout his long rule little if anything was accomplished that altered the life-style of tenants and peasants. Only the conservative ruling class benefited from Haile Selassie's power. In international affairs Haile Selassie was neither all liberal nor all conservative. Although he recognized fascism for what it truly was and tried to warn the world of its ugliness, much of the motivation for doing so stemmed from his own personal insecurity. Though he emerged from Geneva with a liberal and progressive label, his liberality has to be qualified by the personal factors that led him to take the position he did. The same can be said for his involvement with the African continent and particularly his role in the formation of the Organization of African Unity. The 1963 Addis Ababa conference that led to the establishment of the OAU was of great importance to Africa but again Haile Selassie's motivation for entering into political battle with Kwame Nkrumah was in large degree a result of personal factors that had impinged upon the emperor since at least 1894, when his mother died, but certainly since 1906, upon the death of his father, *Ras* Makonnen. This is not to take away from the importance of Haile Selassie as an international statesman but only to put his position into its proper historical framework.

Haile Selassie, buffeted by powerful forces of anxiety that led him to fear helplessness and powerlessness to an abnormal degree, allowed his emotional insecurity to determine his political style and process. The personal factors, already manifest before the twentieth century, are the key to understanding what motivated Haile Selassie throughout his life. It can be said that Haile Selassie did not develop emotionally after the deaths of his parents and he was to an enormous degree a prisoner of his early anxiety due to these deaths. His actions throughout his reign are indication of this. He was caught in a spiderweb of fears that more often than not determined his politics.

Haile Selassie was truly a man of history, a man who, whatever his motivations, struggled against internal and external forces that consistently tried to topple him from power. That

he survived as long as he did and successfully created a positive worldwide image is testimony to his political prowess. He
was a masterful politician and a superb effector of his own
public image. As one Ethiopian who served in his cabinet
said, "he was a wonderful actor."[4] But he was a successful one.
Any leader who can survive in power for fifty-eight years is
worthy of history, and this is particularly so within the intrigue
and complexity of life in Ethiopia. Haile Selassie could be
cruel and kind, conservative and liberal, an autocrat internally
and a liberal internationally. That individuals could simulta-
neously believe and accept all his contradictions is not
difficult to believe when one analyzes his political life. Haile
Selassie could be all things to all people because he showed to
each group only that part of him that would reinforce the
particular image each held of him. That this is almost impossible to do goes without saying; that he did it successfully and
for so long is surprising. He may not have been a great leader
but he was a clever politician that history will enshrine, however tentatively.

Haile Selassie, the Lion of Judah, the emperor whom one
was not permitted to turn his or her back on, and when leaving
his presence had to back away bowing deferentially,[5] composed his own epitaph in 1961: "It is . . . axiomatic that
change begets change, that each step forward leads logically
and inexorably to the next, and the next. Once unleashed, the
forces of history cannot be contained or restrained. . . ."[6]

In the 1970s Emperor Haile Selassie could not grasp the
forces of change that were sweeping Ethiopia and he was
thrust aside by the events of history more powerful than even
the emperor. From a man who created history, he now became
a man of history. At eighty-three years of age, when Haile
Selassie died, an era came to an end, ushered out by the new
centurions of the Third World—the men in military uniform.

The final determination that history will make of Haile
Selassie's rule will be decided in the next decade or two when
those who write history will apply their ideological framework
to an analysis of his reign. Through a slow evolutionary process an image will emerge, rightly or wrongly, that will be
attached to Haile Selassie. History is really what historians
can understand of it, and Haile Selassie within the context of

history will be finally whatever historians can understand of a man who tried to make himself an image. He will be no more and no less.

This biography is written by one who spent large periods of time in the Ethiopia that Haile Selassie led, one who knew some of the people who worked with the emperor, and many more who lived under his rule, and who met and saw the emperor a number of times. Although it is only one book of the many sure to follow, it is written by one who was there and by one who has always been critical, and it is the first biography to emerge after the death of Haile Selassie. And although I have placed Haile Selassie into the psychological and political context that I have perceived to be accurate, only the full weight of history can make a final determination and that judgement must be awaited.

Notes

Scholarly Research on Ethiopia under Haile Selassie's Rule—Chapter 1

1. Alula Hidaru and Dessalegn Rahmato, eds., *A Short Guide to the Study of Ethiopia* (Westport, Conn.: Greenwood, 1976), p. 2.

2. Ibid., p. 3.

3. Christopher Clapham, *Haile-Selassie's Government* (London: Longmans, Green, 1969); Assefa Bequele and Eshetu Chole, *A Profile of the Ethiopian Economy* (London: Oxford University Press, 1969); John Markakis, *Ethiopia, Anatomy of a Traditional Polity* (Oxford: Clarendon Press, 1974); Patrick Gilkes, *The Dying Lion* (London: Julian Friedmann, 1975); Peter Schwab, *Decision Making in Ethiopia* (London: Christopher Hurst, 1972); Margery Perham, *The Government of Ethiopia* (Evanston: Northwestern University Press, 1969).

4. Allan Hoben, *Land Tenure Among the Amhara of Ethiopia* (Chicago: University of Chicago Press, 1973); John M. Cohen, "Ethiopia After Haile Selassie," *African Affairs* 72, no. 289 (October 1973); Paul Brietzke, "Land Reform in Revolutionary Ethiopia," *The Journal of Modern African Studies* 14, no. 4 (1976).

5. Among the best are: Frederick C. Gamst, *The Qemant* (New York: Holt, Rinehart, and Winston, 1969); Herbert S. Lewis, *A Galla Monarchy* (Madison: University of Wisconsin Press, 1965); Donald N. Levine, *Wax and Gold* (Chicago: University of Chicago Press, 1966); William A. Shack, *The Gurage: A People of the Ensete Culture* (New York: Oxford University Press, 1966); Jack Stauder, *The Manjangir* (Cambridge: Cambridge University Press, 1971).

6. Colin Legum, *Ethiopia: The Fall of Haile Selassie's Empire* (New York: Africana, 1975); An Observer, "Revolution in Ethiopia," *Monthly Review* 29 (July–August 1977); John M. Cohen, Arthur A. Goldsmith, and John W. Mellor, "Rural Development Issues Following Ethiopian Land Reform," *Africa Today* 23, no. 2 (April–June 1976); Marina Ottaway, "Social Classes and Corporate Interests in the Ethiopian Revolution," *The Journal of Modern African Studies* 14, no. 3 (1976); Peter Schwab, "Human Rights in Ethiopia," *Journal of Modern African Studies* 14, no. 1 (1976); Peter Schwab, "Rebellion in Gojam Province, Ethiopia," *Canadian Journal of African Studies* 4, no. 2 (Spring 1970).

7. Important are Asmarom Legesse, *Gada: Three Approaches to the Study of African Society* (New York: The Free Press, 1973); Hoben (n. 4); and Levine (n. 5).

8. Marvin Surkin and Alan Wolfe, *An End to Political Science* (New York: Basic Books, 1970), p. 4.

9. For an extensive analysis of the Ethiopian-Somali dispute over the Ogaden and its international ramifications, see Tom J. Farer, *War Clouds on the Horn of Africa* (New York: Carnegie Institute for International Peace, 1976); Peter Schwab, "Cold War on the Horn of Africa," *African Affairs* 77, no. 306 (January 1978).

10. The sole important biographical work is Leonard Mosley, *Haile Selassie: The Conquering Lion* (Englewood Cliffs, N.J.: Prentice-Hall, 1965).

11. Hidaru and Rahmato, *A Short Guide*, p. 4. For a marvelous example of what they are talking about, see the biography written especially for Euro-

pean children: Elizabeth Skinner and James Skinner, *Haile Selassie* (London: Thomas Nelson and Sons, 1967).

12. Robert L. Hess, *Ethiopia, The Modernization of Autocracy* (Ithaca, N.Y.: Cornell University Press, 1970), p. 103.

13. See Appendix A for the full address to the League of Nations.

14. *Public Papers of the Presidents of the United States, John F. Kennedy (1963)* (Washington: United States Government Printing Office, 1964), Document 394, p. 754.

15. Markakis, p. 208.

16. *The 1955 Constitution,* Chapter 1, Articles 2, 4. See also Thomas E. Dow, Jr., "The Theory of Charisma," *Sociological Quarterly* (Summer 1969).

The Ethiopian Context—Chapter 2

1. For the full story of this myth, see A. H. M. Jones and Elizabeth Monroe, *A History of Ethiopia* (Oxford: Clarendon Press, 1966), Part One. Other fine histories covering the period discussed are David Mathew, *Ethiopia, The Study of a Polity 1540–1935* (London: Eyre & Spottiswoode, 1947); Mordechai Abir, *Ethiopia: The Era of the Princes* (New York: Frederick A. Praeger, 1968); H. G. Marcus, *The Life and Times of Menelik II* (Oxford: Clarendon Press, 1974); Richard Pankhurst, *An Introduction to the Economic History of Ethiopia from Early Times to 1800* (London: Lalibela House, 1961).

2. For an introduction to the Falasha, see Wolf Leslau, *Falasha Anthology: The Black Jews of Ethiopia* (New York: Schocken, 1969).

3. For thorough analyses of feudalism in Ethiopia see the following: Gebre-Wold Ingida Worq, "Ethiopia's Traditional System of Land Tenure and Taxation," *Ethiopia Observer* 5, no. 4 (1962); *Land Tenure Surveys of the Provinces of Arussi, Gamu Gofa, Shoa, Sidamo, Wellega, Wello, Eritrea* (Addis Ababa: Ministry of Land Reform and Administration, covering the years 1967–1970); John Markakis, "Social Formation and Political Adaptation in Ethiopia," *Journal of Modern African Studies* 11, no. 3 (1973); Markakis, *Ethiopia, Anatomy of a Traditional Polity* (Oxford: Clarendon Press, 1974), Chapters 4 and 5; Peter Schwab, *Decision Making in Ethiopia* (London: Christopher Hurst, 1972), Chapters 1–4; John M. Cohen, "Ethiopia After Haile Selassie," *African Affairs* 72 (October 1973): 365–82, Richard Pankhurst, "Tribute, Taxation and Government Revenues in Nineteenth and Early Twentieth Century Ethiopia," *Journal of Ethiopian Studies* 5, no. 2 (July 1967).

Prologue: September 12, 1974—Chapter 3

1. *Radio Addis Ababa,* September 12, 1974.

2. Interview with author, August 1967.

The Struggle to Survive—Chapter 4

1. *The Autobiography of Emperor Haile Selassie I,* "My Life and Ethiopia's Progress, 1892–1937," translated and annotated by Edward Ullendorff (Oxford: Oxford University Press, 1976), p. 19.

2. Ibid.
3. Ibid.
4. Ibid., p. 28.
5. Donald N. Levine, *Wax and Gold* (Chicago: University of Chicago Press, 1966), p. 158.
6. C. H. Stigand, *To Abyssinia Through an Unknown Land* (Philadelphia: J. B. Lippincott, 1910), pp. 260–61.
7. Levine, *Wax and Gold*, pp. 156–57.
8. For an analysis of this principle within the context of psychological theory, see E. Furman, *A Child's Parent Dies* (New Haven: Yale University Press, 1974).
9. See *The Autobiography of Emperor Haile Selassie*, Chapters 4–25. For various theories concerning Zauditu's death, see Richard Greenfield, *Ethiopia, A New Political History* (New York: Frederick A. Praeger, 1965), p. 163.
10. Levine, *Wax and Gold*, pp. 135–137.
11. John Markakis, *Ethiopia, Anatomy of a Traditional Polity* (Oxford: Clarendon Press, 1974), pp. 197–98.
12. Levine, *Wax and Gold*, p. 85.
13. *The Autobiography of Emperor Haile Selassie*, p. 25.
14. Markakis, *Ethiopia*, p. 197.
15. *The Autobiography of Emperor Haile Selassie*, p. 29.
16. Ibid.
17. Ibid., p. 34.
18. Irving Kaplan, et al., *Area Handbook for Ethiopia* (Washington: U.S. Government Printing Office, 1971), p. 53.
19. A. H. M. Jones and Elizabeth Monroe, *A History of Ethiopia* (Oxford: Clarendon Press, 1966), p. 160.
20. *The Autobiography of Emperor Haile Selassie*, p. 62.
21. See discussion of this point earlier in this chapter.
22. For the development of this point within the framework of psychology, see R. D. Laing, *The Politics of Experience* (New York: Ballantine, 1970), pp. 25–37.
23. Levine, *Wax and Gold*, p. 76.
24. Richard Greenfield, *Ethiopia, A New Political History* (New York: Frederick A. Praeger, 1965), p. 150.
25. *Selected Speeches of His Imperial Majesty Haile Selassie I, 1918–1967* (Addis Ababa: Ministry of Information, 1967), p. 650.
26. Stigand, *To Abyssinia*, p. 331.

The Coronation of *Ras* Tafari Makonnen—Chapter 5

1. Ellen N. La Motte, "A Coronation in Abyssinia," *Harper's Monthly Magazine* 162 (April 1931): 576.
2. Evelyn Waugh, *When the Going Was Good* (New York: Penguin, 1951), pp. 85–86. See also Gene D. Phillips, *Evelyn Waugh's Officers, Gentlemen, and Rogues* (Chicago: Nelson-Hall, 1975).
3. *The Autobiography of Emperor Haile Selassie*, p. 175.
4. Waugh, *When the Going Was Good*, pp. 91–92.
5. La Motte, *A Coronation*, p. 579.
6. Greenfield, *Ethiopia*, p. 167.
7. La Motte, *A Coronation*, p. 579.

8. Christopher Clapham, *Haile-Selassie's Government* (London: Longmans, Green, 1969), p. 47.

9. *The 1931 Constitution*, Chapter I, Article 3. The full Constitution can be found in Peter Schwab, ed., *Ethiopia and Haile Selassie* (New York: Facts on File Pub., 1972), pp. 12–16.

10. Margery Perham, *The Government of Ethiopia* (Evanston, Ill.: Northwestern University Press, 1948), p. 81.

11. La Motte, *A Coronation*, p. 582.

The Personal Centralization of Power—Chapter 6

1. John Markakis and Asmelash Beyene, "Representative Institutions in Ethiopia," *Journal of Modern African Studies* 5, no. 2 (1967): 201.

2. *The Autobiography of Emperor Haile Selassie*, p. 178.

3. *The 1931 Constitution*.

4. Ibid., Article 5.

5. Markakis, *Anatomy of Ethiopia*, p. 273. There are precisely two studies that extensively analyze the Ethiopian parliament. They are Markakis and Beyene, "Representative Institutions," and Schwab, *Decision Making*. Both deal with parliament as it existed in 1931 and 1955; the latter, in a number of chapters, analyzes the political process within parliament.

6. *The 1931 Constitution*, Articles 50–54.

7. How this contradiction resulted in the overthrow of Haile Selassie in 1974 is analyzed in Peter Schwab, "Haile Selassie: Leadership in Ethiopia," *Plural Societies* 6, no. 2 (1975).

8. Greenfield, *Ethiopia*, p. 176.

9. J. Lee Shneidman, Gabriel Koz, and Conalee Levine-Shneidman, "Catherine de Medicis," *Psychobiography* 1, no. 1 (February 1978): 5.

10. *The Autobiography of Emperor Haile Selassie*, p. 201.

11. Ibid., p. 195. Stated in relation to the *1931 Constitution*.

Denouncing Appeasement: The Conscience of Humanity—Chapter 7

1. Statement by Anthony Eden before the Ninety-first (Extraordinary) Session of the League of Nations Council, April 20, 1936. In *Documents on International Affairs*, Volume II, ed. Stephen Heald (London: Oxford University Press, Humphrey Milford, 1937), p. 450.

2. Ibid., pp. 450–51.

3. Speech of Haile Selassie before League of Nations Assembly, June 30, 1936, *Selected Speeches of His Imperial Majesty Haile Selassie I: 1918–1967* (Addis Ababa: Ministry of Information, 1967). See Appendix A for full speech.

4. Sigmund Neumann, *The Future in Perspective* (New York: G. P. Putnam's Sons, 1946), p. 262.

5. Anthony Eden, *Facing the Dictators* (Boston: Houghton Mifflin, 1962), pp. 412–13. My italics.

6. Emilio de Bono, *The Conquest of an Empire* (London: Cresset Press, 1937), p. 161.

7. Ivone Kirkpatrick, *Mussolini, A Study in Power* (New York: Hawthorne, 1964), pp. 319–20.

8. Denis Mack Smith, *Mussolini's Roman Empire* (New York: Viking, 1976), p. 65.

9. Arnold J. Toynbee, "A Tale of Sin and Nemesis," in *The Ethiopian Crisis: Touchstone of Appeasement?*, ed. Ludwig F. Schaefer (Lexington, Mass.: D. C. Heath, 1961), p. 19.

10. *Selected Speeches*, p. 303. Speech of October 3, 1935.

11. Kirkpatrick, *Mussolini*, p. 331.

12. James Dugan and Laurence Lafore, *Days of Emperor and Clown* (Garden City, N.Y.: Doubleday, 1973), p. 220.

13. Levine, *Wax and Gold*, p. 185.

14. Ibid., p. 38.

15. *The Autobiography of Emperor Haile Selassie*, p. 289.

16. Angelo Del Boca, *The Ethiopian War 1935–1941* (Chicago: University of Chicago Press, 1969), pp. 200–201.

17. Ibid., p. 201, from Theodore Eugene Konovaloff.

18. Dugan and Lafore, *Days*, p. 290.

19. Del Boca, *Ethiopian War*, p. 203.

20. *The Autobiography of Emperor Haile Selassie*, p. 292.

21. John Gunther, *Inside Africa* (New York: Harper & Brothers, 1955), p. 270.

22. Dugan and Lafore, *Days*, p. 303.

23. *The Autobiography of Emperor Haile Selassie*, p. 297.

24. Margaret George, *The Warped Vision: British Foreign Policy 1933–1939* (Pittsburgh: University of Pittsburgh Press, 1965), p. 64.

25. Eden, *Facing the Dictators*, p. 431.

26. Ibid., p. 434.

27. Dugan and Lafore, *Days*, p. 309.

28. Eden, *Facing the Dictators*, p. 437.

29. Ibid.

30. Dugan and Lafore, *Days*, p. 308.

31. Del Boca, *Ethiopian War*, pp. 209–10.

32. Eden, *Facing the Dictators*, p. 437.

33. *The Autobiography of Emperor Haile Selassie*, p. 299.

34. See Appendix A for entire speech.

35. Inis L. Claude, Jr., *Swords into Plowshares* (New York: Random House, 1964), p. 241.

36. *Selected Speeches*, Speech of June 1, 1954, p. 355.

37. Winston S. Churchill, *The Second World War*, Vol. 1, *The Gathering Storm* (London: Cassell, 1950), p. 159.

38. *The London Times*, July 2, 1936.

The Contradictions of Absolute Rule—Chapter 8

1. Christopher Clapham, *Haile Selassie's Government* (London: Longmans, Green, 1969), p. 58.

2. *Selected Speeches*, p. 657.

3. Ibid., p. 332.

4. Ibid., p. 338.

5. *Negarit Gazeta*, Proclamation No. 8 of 1942.

6. H. S. Mann and J. C. D. Lawrance, *Land Taxation in Ethiopia—Summary* (Addis Ababa: Ministry of Finance, 1964), p. 3.

7. Hoben, Allan, *Land Tenure among the Amhara of Ethiopia* (Chicago: University of Chicago Press, 1973), p. 35.

8. See Chapter 2, *The Ethiopian Context.*

9. Mann and Lawrance, p. 6. For a more detailed analysis of the 1942 and 1944 Proclamations, see Schwab, *Decision Making,* Chap. 7.

10. Markakis, *Ethiopia,* pp. 121–22.

11. Proclamation No. 117 of 1951; Legal Notice No. 154 of 1951.

12. Gerhard Colm, "The Ideal Tax System," *Social Research* 7, no. 3 (August 1934): 327.

13. Proclamation No. 60 of 1944.

14. *Ethiopia—Statistical Abstract* (Addis Ababa: Central Statistical Office, 1965), p. 141. The U.S. dollar was then equal to $2.40 in Ethiopian currency.

15. Peter Schwab, "The Tax System of Ethiopia," *American Journal of Economics and Sociology* 29, no. 1 (January 1970): 81.

16. Mann and Lawrance, *Land Taxation,* p. 11.

17. Schwab, *Decision Making,* p. 49.

18. At this time there were twelve provinces; after 1962, fourteen.

19. Decree No. 1 of 1942.

20. Perham, *Government,* p. 90.

21. Schwab, *Decision Making,* pp. 51–54.

22. Order No. 1 of 1943.

23. John Markakis and Asmelash Beyene, "Representative Institutions in Ethiopia," *Journal of Modern African Studies* 5, no. 2 (1967), p. 217.

24. The entire *1955 Constitution* can be found in Peter Schwab, ed., *Ethiopia and Haile Selassie* (New York: Facts on File Publishers, 1972), pp. 61–77.

25. *The Constitution of 1955,* Articles 66–69.

26. Ibid., Art. 71.

27. Clapham, *Haile Selassie's Government,* p. 131.

28. Ibid.; Markakis, *Ethiopia;* Schwab, *Decision Making.*

29. See *Selected Speeches.* One representative example is the emperor's March 1966 speech on Constitutional Reform.

30. Greenfield, *Ethiopia,* p. 298.

The Horn of Africa and the American Connection—Chapter 9

1. William H. Lewis, "How a Defence Planner Looks at Africa," in *Africa: From Mystery to Maze,* ed. Helen Kitchen (Lexington, Mass.: Lexington Books, 1976), p. 293.

2. House of Representatives, *Foreign Assistance Act of 1969: Hearings* (Washington: U.S. Government Printing Office, 1969), pp. 826–28.

3. Markakis, *Ethiopia,* p. 257.

4. Peter Schwab, "Haile Selassie: Leadership in Ethiopia," *Plural Societies* 6, no. 2 (1975): 25; Schwab, "Cold War on the Horn of Africa," *African Affairs* 77, no. 306 (Jan. 1978): 12.

5. Stansfield Turner, "The Naval Balance: Not Just a Numbers Game," *Foreign Affairs* 55, no. 2 (January 1977): 342–43.

6. Statement of James R. Schlesinger, Secretary of Defense, Before the Senate Armed Services Committee, United States Senate, Washington, D. C., June 10, 1975.

7. Ray Vicker, "North Yemen Becomes One of Pivotal Nations in an East-West Tilt," *Wall Street Journal,* June 2, 1977.

8. *U.S. Security Agreements and Commitments Abroad, Ethiopia,* Committee on Foreign Relations, U.S. Senate, Part 8, June 1, 1970.

9. See *A History of Kagnew Station and American Forces in Eritrea*, Information Division, IACS-I, Headquarters, U.S. Army Security Agency, Arlington, Virginia, 1973.

10. See Tom J. Farer, *War Clouds on the Horn of Africa* (New York: Carnegie Endowment for International Peace, 1976), Chap. 2.

11. *U.S. Security Agreements*.

12. Abel Jacob, "Israel's Military Aid to Africa," *Journal of Modern African Studies* 9, no. 2 (August 1971).

13. David D. Laitin, "The Political Economy of Military Rule in Somalia," *Journal of Modern African Studies* 14, no. 3 (1976): 449–50.

14. Schwab, "Cold War on the Horn of Africa." Note also Rex Wingerter, "The United States, the Soviet Union and the Indian Ocean: The Competition for the Third World," *Bulletin of Concerned Asian Scholars* 9, no. 3 (1977).

15. J. Bowyer Bell, *The Horn of Africa* (New York: Crane, Russak, 1973), p. 41.

16. *U.S. Security Agreements*, 1904.

17. See Jack Fuller, "Dateline Diego Garcia: Paved-Over Paradise," *Foreign Policy* 28 (Fall 1977).

18. Schwab, "Cold War on the Horn of Africa," pp. 13–14.

A Man of Africa—Chapter 10

1. *U.S. Security Agreements*, p. 1904.

2. *Selected Speeches*, pp. 189–91.

3. For a full discussion and analysis of Pan-Africanism, see J. Gus Liebenow, "Which Road to Pan-African Unity?" in *Politics in Africa*, ed. Gwendolen M. Carter (New York: Harcourt, Brace & World, 1966); Colin Legum, *Pan-Africanism* (New York: Frederick A. Praeger, 1965).

4. An extended analysis of this issue is found in Crawford Young, *Politics in the Congo* (Princeton: Princeton University Press, 1965).

5. *The African Charter of Casablanca*, Article One (United Nations, 1961).

6. *Charter of the Monrovia Conference*, Principle Six (United Nations, 1961).

7. Colin Legum, *Pan-Africanism*, p. 63.

8. Kwame Nkrumah, *Handbook of Revolutionary Warfare* (New York: International Publishers, 1969), p. 8.

9. *Selected Speeches*, pp. 218–19.

10. Ibid., pp. 241–57.

11. See Appendix B for the full Charter of the Organization of African Unity.

12. Robert L. Hess, *Ethiopia, The Modernization of Autocracy* (Ithaca, N.Y.: Cornell University Press, 1970), p. 236.

13. Julius K. Nyerere, *Freedom and Unity* (London: Oxford University Press, 1967), pp. 216–17. Excerpted from a speech given at the Addis Ababa conference, May 24, 1963.

14. *Selected Speeches*, pp. 259, 262.

15. See Clement Henry Moore, *Politics in North Africa* (Boston: Little, Brown, 1970).

16. For Nkrumah's analysis of these events, see Kwame Nkrumah, *Dark Days in Ghana* (New York: International Publishers, 1968).

17. See Robin Luckham, *The Nigerian Military* (Cambridge: Cambridge

University Press, 1971); Peter Schwab, *Biafra* (New York: Facts on File Publishers, 1971).

18. *New York Times*, August 28, 1975.

19. Colin Legum, *Ethiopia: The Fall of Haile Selassie's Empire* (New York: Africana, 1975), p. 49. Statement of President Gaafar Numeiry of the Sudan.

Haile Selassie as Father, Asfa Wossen as Son—Chapter 11

1. Hess, *Ethiopia*, p. 241.

2. *Selected Speeches*, p. 646. Speech given March 18, 1957.

3. Greenfield, *Ethiopia*, p. 206.

4. Ibid., p. 399.

5. Ibid., pp. 336–58. See also Christopher Clapham, "The December 1960 Ethiopian Coup d'Etat," *The Journal of Modern African Studies* 6, no. 4 (1968).

6. Interview by Ethiopianists with Crown Prince Asfa Wossen, August 1967.

7. Patrick Gilkes, *The Dying Lion* (London: Julian Friedman, 1975), p. 267.

8. *Selected Speeches*.

The Whirlwind of Rebellion—Chapter 12

1. Proclamation No. 255 of 1967.

2. *The Ethiopian Herald*, November 23, 1967.

3. See Schwab, *Decision Making*, pp. 98–140.

4. *The 1955 Constitution*, Article 34.

5. Schwab, *Decision Making*, p. 105.

6. Ibid., Chapters 5, 6.

7. Ibid., Chapters 7, 9.

8. Hoben, pp. 217–22; Schwab, *Decision Making*, pp. 158–69; Schwab, "Rebellion in Gojam Province, Ethiopia."

9. *Ethiopian Herald*, August 3, 1968.

Revolution and the Fall from Power—Chapter 13

1. Legum, *Ethiopia*, p. 30.

2. See Jack Shepherd, *The Politics of Starvation* (New York: Carnegie Endowment for International Peace, 1975).

3. Legum, *Ethiopia*, p. 30.

4. For a complete listing of those who were executed, see the *New York Times*, November 25, 1974.

5. Raph Uwechue's interview with Mengistu Haile Mariam, "Our Fight Is With Those Opposed to the Masses," *Africa* (March 1978): 16. For a legal discussion of the executions, see Schwab, "Human Rights in Ethiopia," *Journal of Modern African Studies* 14, no. 1 (1976): 155–60. For an overall discussion of the issue of human rights in Ethiopia, see David Hamilton and Mara Whitcombe, "Discrimination in Ethiopia," in *Case Studies on Human*

Rights and Fundamental Freedoms, ed. Willem A. Veenhoven (The Hague: Martinus Nijhoff, 1976).

6. Prior to and after the 1974 coup, many of the military participants read many of these books. This was made obvious to me in March 1978 during a conversation with one of the editors of the British journal *New Left Review*, who had just returned from interviewing some of the leaders of the Dergue.

7. See *Dialogue*, a publication of the Ethiopian University Teachers' Association (Addis Ababa, April 1968). Note also Schwab, *Decision Making*, pp. 150–57.

8. For an analysis of the outbreak of the revolution and the transformation of the ruling structure, see David Ottaway and Marina Ottaway, *Ethiopia, Empire in Revolution* (New York: Africana, 1978).

9. Legum, *Ethiopia*.

10. See Shepherd, *Politics*.

11. Schwab, *Decision Making*, p. 182.

12. See the years 1974–1978 of the *New York Times*. See also An Observer, "Revolution in Ethiopia," *Monthly Review* 29 (July-August 1977).

13. Legum, *Ethiopia*, p. 49.

History Will Judge—Chapter 14

1. As related to the author by a military officer who was there at the time.

2. Ibid.

3. For a listing of what happened to those who worked with the emperor for years, see previous chapter. See also Legum, *Ethiopia*, and David Ottaway and Marina Ottaway, *Ethiopia, Empire in Revolution*.

4. Statement made by Zewde Gabre-Selassie, April 14, 1978.

5. For a marvelous and amusing description, see David Holden, "Ethiopia—Forty Years On," *Encounter* (February 1973), p. 87.

6. *Selected Speeches*, p. 410. Emperor's statement to government officials, April 14, 1961.

Appendix A
Text of Haile Selassie's Address
to the League of Nations,
June 30, 1936

Source: *Selected Speeches of His Imperial Majesty Haile Selassie I: 1918–1967*. Addis Ababa Ministry of Information, 1967. (Translated by the Ministry of Information.) Pp. 304–316.

I, Haile Selassie I, emperor of Ethiopia, am here today to claim that justice which is due to my people, and the assistance promised to it eight months ago, when fifty nations asserted that aggression had been committed in violation of international treaties.

There is no precedent for a head of state himself speaking in this Assembly. But there is also no precedent for a people being victim of such injustice, and being at present threatened by abandonment to its aggressor. Also, there has never before been an example by any government proceeding to the systematic extermination of a nation by barbarous means in violation of the most solemn promises made by the nations of the earth that there should not be used against innocent human beings the terrible poison of harmful gases. It is to defend a people struggling for its age-old independence that the head of the Ethiopian empire has come to Geneva to fulfill this supreme duty, after having himself fought at the head of his armies.

I pray to Almighty God that He may spare nations the terrible sufferings that have just been inflicted on my people and of which the chiefs who accompany me here have been the horrified witnesses. It is my duty to inform the governments assembled in Geneva, responsible as they are for the lives of millions of men, women, and children, of the deadly peril which threatens them, by describing to them the fate which has been suffered by Ethiopia.

It is not only upon warriors that the Italian government has made war. It has above all attacked populations far removed from hostilities, in order to terrorize and exterminate them.

At the beginning, towards the end of 1935, Italian aircraft hurled upon my armies bombs of tear-gas. Their effects were but slight. The soldiers learned to scatter, waiting until the wind had rapidly dispersed the poisonous gases. The Italian aircraft then resorted to mustard gas. Barrels of liquid were hurled upon armed groups. But this means also was not effective. The liquid affected only a few soldiers and barrels upon the ground were themselves a warning to troops and to the population of the danger.

It was at the time when the operations for the encircling of Makalle [in northern Ethiopia] were taking place that the Italian command, fearing a rout, followed the procedure which it is now my duty to denounce to the world. Special sprayers were installed on board aircraft so that they could vaporize, over vast areas of territory, a fine, death-dealing rain. Groups of 9, 15, 18 aircraft followed one another so that the fog issuing from them formed a continuous sheet. It was thus that, as from the end of January 1936, soldiers, women, children, cattle, rivers, lakes and pastures were drenched continually with this deadly rain. In order to kill off systematically all living creatures, in order the more surely to poison waters and pastures, the Italian command made its aircraft pass over and over again. That was its chief method of warfare.

The very refinement of barbarism consisted in carrying ravage and terror into the most densely populated parts of the territory, the points farthest removed from the scene of hostilities. The object was to scatter fear and death over a great part of the Ethiopian territory.

These fearful tactics succeeded. Men and animals succumbed. The deadly rain that fell from the aircraft made all those whom it touched fly shrieking with pain. All those who drank the poisoned water or ate the infected food also succumbed in dreadful suffering. In tens of thousands, the victims of the Italian mustard gas fell. It is in order to denounce to the civilized world the tortures inflicted upon the Ethiopian people that I resolved to come to Geneva.

None other than myself and my brave companions in arms could bring the League of Nations the undeniable proof. The appeals of my delegates addressed to the League of Nations had remained without any answer; my delegates had not been witnesses. That is why I decided to come myself to bear witness against the crime perpetrated against my people and give Europe a warning of the doom that awaits it, if it should bow before the accomplished fact.

Is it necessary to remind the Assembly of the various stages of the Ethiopian drama? For 20 years past either as heir apparent, regent of the empire, or as emperor, I have never ceased to use all my efforts to bring my country the benefits of civilization, and in particular to establish relations of good neighborliness with adjacent powers. In particular I succeeded in concluding with Italy the Treaty of Friendship of 1928, which absolutely prohibited the resort, under any pretext whatsoever, to force of arms, substituting for force and pressure the conciliation and arbitration on which civilized nations have based international order.

In its report of October 5, 1935, the Committee of 13 [of the League] recognized my effort and the results that I achieved. The governments thought that the entry of Ethiopia into the League, whilst giving that country a new guarantee for the maintenance of her territorial integrity and independence, would help her to reach a higher level of civilization. It does not seem that in Ethiopia today there is more disorder and insecurity than in 1923. On the contrary, the country is more united and the central power is better obeyed.

I should have procured still greater results for my people if obstacles of every kind had not been put in the way by the Italian government, the government which stirred up revolt and armed the rebels. Indeed the

Rome government, as it has today openly proclaimed, has never ceased to prepare for the conquest of Ethiopia. The treaties of friendship it signed with me were not sincere; their only object was to hide its real intention from me. The Italian government asserts that for fourteen years it has been preparing for its present conquest. It therefore recognizes today that when it supported the admission of Ethiopia to the League of Nations in 1923, when it concluded the Treaty of Friendship in 1928, when it signed the pact of Paris outlawing war, it was deceiving the whole world.

The Ethiopian government was, in these solemn treaties, given additional guarantees of security which would enable it to achieve further progress along the pacific path of reform on which it had set its feet and to which it was devoting all its strength and all its heart.

The Walwal incident, in December 1934, came as a thunderbolt to me. The Italian provocation was obvious, and I did not hesitate to appeal to the League of Nations. I invoked the provisions of the treaty of 1928, the principles of the covenant [of the League]; I urged the procedure of conciliation and arbitration.

Unhappily for Ethiopia, this was the time when a certain government considered that the European situation made it imperative at all costs to obtain the friendship of Italy. The price paid was the abandonment of Ethiopian independence to the greed of the Italian government. This secret agreement [of January 1935, between Britain and Italy, recognizing Italian influence over Ethiopia], contrary to the obligations of the covenant, has exerted a great influence over the course of events. Ethiopia and the whole world have suffered and are still suffering today its disastrous consequences.

This first violation of the covenant was followed by many others. Feeling itself encouraged in its policy against Ethiopia, the Rome government feverishly made war preparations thinking that the concerted pressure which was beginning to be exerted on the Ethiopian government might perhaps not overcome the resistance of my people to Italian domination.

The time had to come, thus all sorts of difficulties were placed in the way with a view to breaking up the procedure of conciliation and arbitration. All kinds of obstacles were placed in the way of that procedure. Governments tried to prevent the Ethiopian government from finding arbitrators amongst their nationals: when once the arbitral tribunal was set up, pressure was exercised so that an award favorable to Italy should be given. All this was in vain: the arbitrators—two of whom were Italian officials—were forced to recognize unanimously that in the Walwal incident, as in the subsequent incidents, no international responsibility was to be attributed to Ethiopia.

Following on this award, the Ethiopian government sincerely thought that an era of friendly relations might be opened with Italy. I loyally offered my hand to the Rome government.

The Assembly was informed by the report of the Committee of

Thirteen, dated October 5, 1935, of the details of the events which
occurred after the month of December 1934 and up to October 3,
1935. It will be sufficient if I quote a few of the conclusions of that
report (Nos. 24, 25, and 26): The Italian memorandum (containing the
complaints made by Italy) was laid on the Council table on September 4, 1935, whereas Ethiopia's first appeal to the Council had
been made on December 14, 1934. In the interval between these two
dates, the Italian government opposed the consideration of the question by the Council on the ground that the only appropriate procedure was that provided for in the Italo-Ethiopian Treaty of 1928.
Throughout the whole of that period, moreover, the dispatch of Italian troops to East Africa was proceeding. These shipments of troops
were represented to the Council by the Italian government as necessary for the defense of its colonies menaced by Ethiopia's preparations. Ethiopia, on the contrary, drew attention to the official pro-
nouncements made in Italy which, in its opinion, left no doubt "as to
the hostile intentions of the Italian government."

From the outset of the dispute, the Ethiopian government has
sought a settlement by peaceful means. It has appealed to the procedures of the covenant. The Italian government desiring to keep
strictly to the procedures of the Italo-Ethiopian Treaty of 1928, the
Ethiopian government assented. It invariably stated that it would
faithfully carry out the arbitral award even if the decision went
against it. It agreed that the question of the ownership of Walwal
should not be dealt with by the arbitrators, because the Italian government would not agree to such a course. It asked the Council to
dispatch neutral observers and offered to lend itself to any inquiries
upon which the Council might decide.

Once the Walwal dispute had been settled by arbitration, however,
the Italian government submitted its detailed memorandum to the
Council in support of its claim to liberty of action. It asserted that a
case like that of Ethiopia cannot be settled by the means provided by
the covenant. It stated that, "since this question affects vital interests
and is of primary importance to Italian security and civilization," it
"would be failing in its most elementary duty, did it not cease once
and for all to place any confidence in Ethiopia reserving full liberty to
adopt any measures that may become necessary to ensure the safety
of its colonies and to safeguard its own interests."

Those are the terms of the report of the Committee of Thirteen.
The Council and the Assembly unanimously adopted the conclusion
that the Italian government had violated the covenant and was in a
state of aggression.

I did not hesitate to declare that I did not wish for war, that it was
imposed upon me, and I should struggle solely for the independence
and integrity of my people, and that in that struggle I was the defend-
er of the cause of all small states exposed to the greed of a powerful
neighbor.

In October 1935, the fifty-two nations who are listening to me today gave me an assurance that the aggressor would not triumph, that the resources of the covenant would be employed in order to ensure the reign of right and the failure of violence. I ask the fifty-two nations not to forget today the policy upon which they embarked eight months ago, and on faith of which I directed the resistance of my people against the aggressor whom they had denounced to the world. Despite the inferiority of my weapons, the complete lack of aircraft, artillery, munitions, hospital services, my confidence in the League was absolute. I thought it to be impossible that fifty-two nations, including the most powerful in the world, should be successfully opposed by a single aggressor. Counting on the faith due to treaties, I had made no preparation for war, and that is the case with certain small countries in Europe.

When the danger became more urgent, being aware of my responsibilities towards my people, during the first six months of 1935 I tried to acquire armaments. Many governments proclaimed an embargo to prevent my doing so, whereas the Italian government, through the Suez Canal, was given all facilities for transporting, without cessation and without protest, troops, arms and munitions.

On October 3, 1935, the Italian troops invaded my territory. A few hours later only I decreed general mobilization. In my desire to maintain peace I had, following the example of a great country in Europe on the eve of the Great War, caused my troops to withdraw 30 kilometers so as to remove any pretext of provocation.

War then took place in the atrocious conditions which I have laid before the Assembly. In that unequal struggle between a government commanding more than 42 million inhabitants, having at its disposal financial, industrial and technical means which enabled it to create unlimited quantities of the most death-dealing weapons, and, on the other hand, a small people of 12 million inhabitants, without arms, without resources, having on its side only the justice of its own cause and the promise of the League of Nations, what real assistance was given to Ethiopia by the fifty-two nations who have declared the Rome government guilty of a breach of the covenant and had undertaken to prevent the triumph of the aggressor? Has each of the states members, as it was its duty to do in virtue of its signature appended to Article 15 of the covenant, considered the aggressor as having committed an act of war personally directed against itself? I had placed all my hopes in the execution of these undertakings. My confidence had been confirmed by the repeated declarations made in Council to the effect that aggression must not be rewarded, and that force would end by being compelled to bow before right.

In December 1935 the Council made it quite clear that its feelings were in harmony with those of hundreds of millions of people who, in all parts of the world, had protested against the proposals to dismember Ethiopia. It was constantly repeated that there was not merely a conflict between the Italian government and the League of Nations, and that is why I personally refused all proposals to my personal advantage made to me by the Italian government, if only I would betray my people and the covenant of the League of Nations. I was defending the cause of all small peoples who are threatened with aggression.

What have become of the promises made to me as long ago as October 1935? I noted with grief, but without surprise, that three powers considered their undertakings under the covenant as absolutely of no value. Their connections with Italy impelled them to refuse to take any measures whatsoever in order to stop Italian aggression. On the contrary, it was a profound disappointment to me to learn the attitude of a certain government which, whilst ever protesting its scrupulous attachment to the covenant, has tirelessly used all its efforts to prevent its observance. As soon as any measure which was likely to be rapidly effective was proposed, various pretexts were devised in order to postpone even consideration of the measure. Did the secret agreements of January 1935 provide for this tireless obstruction?

The Ethiopian government never expected other governments to shed their soldiers' blood to defend the covenant when their own immediately personal interests were not at stake. Ethiopian warriors asked only for means to defend themselves. On many occasions I have asked for financial assistance for the purchase of arms. That assistance has been constantly refused me. What, then, in practice, is the meaning of Article 16 of the covenant and of collective security?

The Ethiopian government's use of the railway from Djibouti to Addis Ababa was in practice hampered as regards transport of arms intended for the Ethiopian forces. At the present moment this is the chief, if not the only, means of supply of the Italian armies of occupation. The rules of neutrality should have prohibited transports intended for Italian forces, but there is not even neutrality since Article 16 lays upon every state member of the League the duty not to remain a neutral but to come to the aid not of the aggressor but of the victim of aggression. Has the covenant been respected? Is it today being respected?

Finally a statement has just been made in their parliaments by the governments of certain powers, amongst them the most influential members of the League of Nations, that since the aggressor has succeeded in occupying a large part of Ethiopian territory, they propose not to continue the application of any economic and financial measures that may have been decided upon against the Italian government.

These are the circumstances in which, at the request of the Argentine government, the Assembly of the League of Nations meets to consider the situation created by Italian aggression.

I assert that the problem submitted to the Assembly today is a much wider one. It is not merely a question of the settlement of Italian aggression. It is collective security: it is the very existence of the League of Nations. It is the confidence that each state is to place in international treaties. It is the value of promises made to small states that their integrity and their independence shall be respected and ensured. It is the principle of the equality of states on the one hand, or otherwise the obligation laid upon small powers to accept the bonds of vassalship. In a word, it is international morality that is at stake. Have the signatures appended to a treaty value only in so far as the signatory powers have a personal, direct and immediate interest involved?

No subtlety can change the problem or shift the grounds of the discussion. It is in all sincerity that I submit these considerations to the Assembly. At a time when my people are threatened with extermination, when the support of the League may ward off the final blow, may I be allowed to speak with complete frankness, without reticence, in all directness such as is demanded by the rule of equality as between all states members of the League?

Apart from the Kingdom of the Lord, there is not on this earth any nation that is superior to any other. Should it happen that a strong government finds it may with impunity destroy a weak people, then the hour strikes for that weak people to appeal to the League of Nations to give its judgment in all freedom. God and history will remember your judgment.

I have heard it asserted that the inadequate sanctions already applied have not achieved their object. At no time, and under no circumstances, could sanctions that were intentionally inadequate, intentionally badly applied, stop an aggressor. This is not a case of the impossibility of stopping an aggressor, but of the refusal to stop an aggressor. When Ethiopia requested and requests that she should be given financial assistance, was that a measure which it was impossible to apply whereas financial assistance of the League has been granted, even in times of peace, to two countries and exactly to two countries who have refused to apply sanctions against the aggressor?

Faced by numerous violations by the Italian government of all international treaties that prohibit resort to arms and the use of barbarous methods of warfare, it is my painful duty to note that the initiative has today been taken with a view to raising sanctions. Does this initiative not mean in practice the abandonment of Ethiopia to the aggressor? On the very eve of the day when I was about to attempt a supreme effort in the defense of my people before this Assembly, does not this initiative deprive Ethiopia of one of her last chances to succeed in obtaining the support and guarantee of states members? Is that the guidance the League of Nations and each of the states members are entitled to expect from the great powers when they assert their right and their duty to guide the action of the League?

Placed by the aggressor face to face with the accomplished fact, are states going to set up the terrible precedent of bowing before force?

Your Assembly will doubtless have laid before it proposals for the reform of the covenant and for rendering more effective the guarantee of collective security. Is it the covenant that needs reform? What undertakings can have any value if the will to keep them is lacking? Is it international morality which is at stake and not the articles of the covenant?

On behalf of the Ethiopian people, a member of the League of Nations, I request the Assembly to take all measures proper to ensure respect for the covenant. I renew my protest against the violations of treaties of which the Ethiopian people has been the victim. I declare in the face of the whole world that the emperor, the government, and the people of Ethiopia will not bow before force; that they maintain their claims that they will use all means in their power to ensure the triumph of right and the respect of the covenant.

I ask the fifty-two nations, who have given the Ethiopian people a promise to help them in their resistance to the aggressor, what are they willing to do for Ethiopia? And the great powers who have promised the guarantee of collective security to small states on whom weighs the threat that they may one day suffer the fate of Ethiopia, I ask what measures do you intend to take?

Representatives of the world, I have come to Geneva to discharge in your midst the most painful of the duties of the head of a state. What reply shall I have to take back to my people?

Appendix B
Charter of the Organization of African Unity (May 25, 1963)

Source: *The Organization of African and Malagasy States*. Addis Ababa, May 25, 1963. (Published in English.)

We, the Heads of African and Malagasy States and Governments assembled in the city of Addis Ababa, Ethiopia;

Convinced that it is the inalienable right of all people to control their own destiny;

Conscious of the fact that freedom, equality, justice and dignity are essential objectives for the achievement of the legitimate aspirations of the African peoples;

Conscious of our responsibility to harness the natural and human resources of our continent for the total advancement of our peoples in spheres of human endeavour;

Inspired by a common determination to promote understanding and collaboration among our States in response to the aspirations of our peoples for brotherhood and solidarity, in a larger unity transcending ethnic and national differences;

Convinced that, in order to translate this determination into a dynamic force in the cause of human progress, conditions for peace and security must be established and maintained;

Determined to safeguard and consolidate the hard-won independence as well as the sovereignty and territorial integrity of our States, and to resist neo-colonialism in all its forms;

Dedicated to the general progress of Africa;

Persuaded that the Charter of the United Nations and the Universal Declaration of Human Rights, to the principles of which we reaffirm our adherence, provide a solid foundation for peaceful and positive co-operation among States;

Desirous that all African and Malagasy States should henceforth unite so that the welfare and well-being of their peoples can be assured;

Resolved to reinforce the links between our States by establishing and strengthening common institutions;

Have agreed to the present Charter.

Establishment
Article I

The High Contracting Parties do by the present Charter establish an Organization to be known as the "Organization of African and Malagasy States."

Purposes
Article II

1. The Organization shall have the following purposes:

a. To promote the unity and solidarity of the African and Malagasy States.

b. To co-ordinate and intensify their collaboration and efforts to achieve a better life for the peoples of Africa.

c. To defend their sovereignty, their territorial integrity and independence.

d. To eradicate all forms of colonialism from the continent of Africa; and

e. To promote international co-operation, having due regard to the Charter of the United Nations and the Universal Declaration of Human Rights.

2. To these ends, the Member States shall co-ordinate and harmonise their general policies, especially in the following fields:

a. Political and diplomatic co-operation.

b. Economic co-operation, including transport and communications.

c. Educational and cultural co-operation.

d. Health, sanitation and nutritional co-operation.

e. Scientific and technical co-operation.

f. Co-operation for defence and security.

Principles
Article III

The Member States, in pursuit of the purposes stated in Article II, solemnly affirm, and declare their adherence to the following principles:

1. The sovereign equality of all African and Malagasy States.

2. Non-interference in the internal affairs of States.

3. Respect for the sovereignty and territorial integrity of each State and for its inalienable right to independent existence.

4. Peaceful settlement of disputes by negotiation, mediation, conciliation or arbitration.

5. Unreserved condemnation, in all its forms, of political assassination as well as subversive activities on the part of neighboring States or any other States.

6. Absolute dedication to the whole emancipation of the African territories which are still dependent.

7. Affirmation of a policy of non-alignment with regard to all blocs.

Membership
Article IV

Each independent sovereign African and Malagasy State shall be entitled to become a Member of the Organization.

Rights and Duties of Member States
Article V

All Member States shall enjoy equal rights and have equal duties.

Article VI

The Member States pledge themselves to observe scrupulously the principles enumerated in Article III of the present Charter.

Institutions
Article VII

The Organization shall accomplish its purposes through the following principal institutions:
1. The Assembly of Heads of State and Government.
2. The Council of Ministers.
3. The General Secretariat.
4. The Commission of Mediation, Conciliation and Arbitration.

The Assembly of Heads of State and Government
Article VIII

The Assembly of Heads of State and Government shall be the supreme organ of the Organization. It shall, subject to the provisions of this Charter, discuss matters of common concern to all Member States with a view to co-ordinating and harmonising the general policy of the Organization. It may in addition review the structure, functions and acts of all the organs and any specialized agencies which may be created in accordance with the present Charter.

Article IX

The Assembly shall be composed of the Heads of State and Government or their duly accredited representatives and it shall meet at least once a year (every other year). At the request of any Member State, and approval by the majority of the Member States, the Assembly shall meet in extraordinary session.

Article X

1. Each Member State shall have one vote.
2. All resolutions shall be determined by a two-thirds majority of those present and voting.
3. Questions of procedure shall require a simple majority. Whether or not a question is one of procedure shall be determined by a simple majority of all Member States present and voting.
4. Two-thirds of the total membership of the Organization shall form a quorum at any meeting of the Assembly.

Article XI

The Assembly shall have the power to determine its own rules of procedure.

The Council of Ministers
Article XII

The Council of Ministers shall consist of Foreign Ministers or such other Ministers as are designated by the Governments of Member States.

The Council of Ministers shall meet at least twice a year. When requested by any Member State and approved by two-thirds of all Member States, it shall meet in extraordinary session.

Article XIII

The Council of Ministers shall be responsible to the Assembly of Heads of State and Government. It shall be entrusted with the responsibility of preparing conferences of the Assembly.

It shall take cognisance of any matter referred to it by the Assembly. It shall be entrusted with the implementation of the decisions of the Assembly of Heads of State. It shall co-ordinate inter-African co-operation in accordance with the instructions of the Assembly and in conformity with Article II (2) of the present Charter.

Article XIV

1. Each Member State shall have one vote.

2. All resolutions shall be determined by a two-thirds majority of those members present and voting.

3. Questions of procedure shall require a simple majority. Whether or not a question is one of procedure shall be determined by a simple majority of all Member States present and voting.

4. Two-thirds of the total membership of the Council shall form a quorum for any meeting of the Council.

Article XV

The Council shall have the power to determine its own rules of procedure.

General Secretariat
Article XVI

There shall be an Administrative Secretary-General of the Organization, who shall be appointed by the Assembly of Heads of State and Government, on the recommendation of the Council of Ministers. The Administrative Secretary-General shall direct the affairs of the Secretariat.

Article XVII

There shall be one or more Assistant Secretaries-General of the Organization, who shall be appointed by the Council of Ministers.

Article XVIII

The functions and conditions of services of the Secretary-General, of the Assistant Secretaries-General and other employees of the Secretariat shall be governed by the provisions of this Charter and the regulations approved by the Council of Ministers.

1. In the performance of their duties the Administrative Secretary-General and his staff shall not seek or receive instructions from any government or from any other authority external to the Organization. They shall refrain from any action which might reflect on their position as international officials responsible only to the Organization.

2. Each member of the Organization undertakes to respect the exclusive character of the responsibilities of the Administrative Secretary-General and the Staff and not seek to influence them in the discharge of their responsibilities.

Commission of Mediation, Conciliation and Arbitration
Article XIX

Member States pledge to settle all disputes among themselves by peaceful means and, to this end, agree to conclude a separate treaty establishing a Commission of Mediation, Conciliation and Arbitration. Said treaty shall be regarded as forming an integral part of the present Charter [done July 21, 1964, in Cairo].

Specialized Commissions
Article XX

The Assembly shall establish such Specialized Commissions as it may deem necessary, including the following:

1. Economic and Social Commission.
2. Educational and Cultural Commission.
3. Health, Sanitation and Nutrition Commission.
4. Defence Commission.
5. Scientific, Technical and Research Commission.

Article XXI

Each Specialized Commission referred to in Article XX shall be composed of the Ministers concerned or other Ministers or Plenipotentiaries designated by the Governments of the Member States.

Article XXII

The functions of the Specialized Commissions shall be carried out in accordance with the provisions of the present Charter and of the regulations approved by the Council of Ministers.

The Budget
Article XXIII

The budget of the Organization prepared by the Administrative Secretary-General shall be approved by the Council of Ministers. The budget shall be provided by contributions from Member States in accordance with the scale of assessment of the United Nations; provided, however, that no Member State shall be assessed an amount exceeding twenty per cent of the yearly regular budget of the Organization. The Member States agree to pay their respective contributions regularly.

Signature and Ratification of Charter
Article XXIV

This Charter shall be open for signature to all independent sovereign African and Malagasy States and shall be ratified by the signatory States in accordance with their respective constitutional processes.

The original instrument, done in English and French, both texts being equally authentic, shall be deposited with the Government of Ethiopia which shall transmit certified copies thereof to all independent sovereign African and Malagasy States.

Instruments of ratification shall be deposited with the Government of Ethiopia, which shall notify all signatories of each such deposit.

Entry into Force
Article XXV

The Charter shall enter into force immediately upon receipt by the Government of Ethiopia of the instruments of ratification from two-thirds of the signatory States.

Registration of the Charter
Article XXVI

This Charter shall, after due ratification, be registered with the Secretariat of the United Nations through the Government of Ethiopia in conformity with Article 102 of the Charter of the United Nations.

Interpretation of the Charter
Article XXVII

Any question which may arise concerning the interpretation of this Charter shall be decided by a vote of two-thirds of the Assembly of Heads of State and Government, present and voting.

Adhesion and Accession
Article XXVIII

1. Any independent sovereign African State may at any time notify the Administrative Secretary-General of its intention to adhere or accede to this Charter.

2. The Administrative Secretary-General shall, on receipt of such notification, communicate a copy of it to all the Member States. Admission shall be decided by a simple majority of the Member States. The decision of each Member State shall be transmitted to the Administrative Secretary-General, who shall, upon receipt of the required number of votes, communicate the decision to the State concerned.

Miscellaneous
Article XXIX

The working languages of the Organization and all its institutions shall be English and French.

Article XXX

The Administrative Secretary-General may accept on behalf of the Organization gifts, bequests and other donations made to the Organization, provided that this is approved by the Council of Ministers.

Article XXXI

The Council of Ministers shall decide on the privileges and immunities to be accorded to the personnel of the Secretariat in the respective territories of the Member States.

Cessation of Membership
Article XXXII

Any State which desires to renounce its membership shall forward a written notification to the Administrative Secretary-General. At the end of one year from the date of such notification, the Charter shall cease to apply with respect to the renouncing State, which shall thereby cease to belong to the Organization.

Amendment to the Charter
Article XXXIII

This Charter may be amended or revised if any Member State makes a written request to the Administrative Secretary-General to that effect; provided, however, that the proposed amendment is not submitted to the Assembly for consideration until all the Member States have been duly notified of it and a period of one year has elapsed. Such an amendment shall not be effective unless approved by at least two-thirds of all the Member States.

In faith whereof, We, the Heads of African and Malagasy States and Governments, have signed this Charter.

Done in the city of Addis Ababa, the 25th day of May, 1963.

[Signatories of the Charter are listed in Chapter 10 of the text]

Bibliography

Books and Articles

Abir, Mordechai. *Ethiopia: The Era of the Princes*. New York: Frederick A. Praeger, 1968.

The Autobiography of Emperor Haile Selassie I, "My Life and Ethiopia's Progress, 1892–1937," translated and annotated by Edward Ullendorff. Oxford: Oxford University Press, 1976.

Bell, J. Bowyer. *The Horn of Africa*. New York: Crane, Russak, 1973.

Bequele, Assefa, and Chole, Eshetu. *A Profile of the Ethiopian Economy*. London: Oxford University Press, 1969.

Brietzke, Paul. "Land Reform in Revolutionary Ethiopia." *The Journal of Modern African Studies* 14, no. 4 (1976): 637–660.

Churchill, Winston S. *The Second World War: The Gathering Storm*. London: Cassell, 1950.

Clapham, Christopher. *Haile-Selassie's Government*. London: Longmans, Green, 1969.

―――. "The December 1960 Coup d'Etat." *The Journal of Modern African Studies* 6, no. 4 (1968): 495–508.

Claude, Inis L., Jr. *Swords Into Plowshares*. New York: Random House, 1964.

Cohen, John M. "Ethiopia After Haile Selassie." *African Affairs* 72, no. 289 (October 1973): 365–382.

Cohen, John M.; Goldsmith, Arthur A.; and Mellor, John W. "Rural Development Issues Following Ethiopian Land Reform." *Africa Today* 23, no. 2 (April–June 1976): 7–28.

Colm, Gerhard. "The Ideal Tax System." *Social Research* 1, no. 3 (August 1934): 319–342.

de Bono, Emilo. *The Conquest of an Empire*. London: Cresset, 1937.

Del Boca, Angelo. *The Ethiopian War 1935–1941*. Chicago: The University of Chicago Press, 1969.

Dialogue. A Publication of the Ethiopian Teachers' Association. Addis Ababa (April 1968).

Dow, Thomas E., Jr. "The Theory of Charisma." *Sociological Quarterly* (Summer 1969): pp. 306–318.

Dugan, James, and LaFore, Laurence. *Days of Emperor and Clown*. Garden City: Doubleday, 1973.

Eden, Anthony. *Facing the Dictators*. Boston: Houghton Mifflin, 1962.

Farer, Tom J. *War Clouds on the Horn of Africa*. New York: Carnegie Endowment for International Peace, 1976.

Friedländer, Saul. *History and Psychoanalysis*. New York: Holmes & Meier, 1978.

Fuller, Jack. "Dateline Diego Garcia: Paved Over Paradise." *Foreign Policy* 28 (Fall 1977): 175–186.

Furman, E. *A Child's Parent Dies*. New Haven: Yale University Press, 1974.

Gamst, Frederick C. *The Qemant*. New York: Holt, Rinehart and Winston, 1969.

Gebre-Wold Ingida Worq. "Ethiopia's Traditional System of Land Tenure and Taxation." *Ethiopia Observer* 5, no. 4 (1962): 302–339.

George, Margaret. *The Warped Vision: British Foreign Policy 1933–1939*. Pittsburgh: The University of Pittsburgh Press, 1965.

Gilkes, Patrick. *The Dying Lion*. London: Julian Friedmann, 1975.

Greenfield, Richard. *Ethiopia, A New Political History*. New York: Frederick A. Praeger, 1965.

Gunther, John. *Inside Africa.* New York: Harper and Brothers, 1955.

Hamilton, David, and Whitcombe, Mara. "Discrimination in Ethiopia." In *Case Studies on Human Rights and Fundamental Freedoms*, edited by Willem A. Veenhoven, pp. 275–302. The Hague: Martinus Nijhoff, 1976.

Hess, Robert L. *Ethiopia, The Modernization of Autocracy.* Ithaca, N.Y.: Cornell University Press, 1970.

Hidaru, Alula, and Rahmato, Dessalegn, editors. *A Short Guide to the Study of Ethiopia.* Westport, Conn.: Greenwood, 1976.

Hoben, Allan. *Land Tenure Among the Amhara of Ethiopia.* Chicago: The University of Chicago Press, 1973.

Holden, David. "Ethiopia—Forty Years On." *Encounter* (February 1973): pp. 76–87.

Jacob, Abel. "Israel's Military Aid to Africa." *The Journal of Modern African Studies* 9, no. 2 (1971): 165–187.

Jesman, Czeslaw. *The Ethiopian Paradox.* London: Oxford University Press, 1963.

Jones, A. H. M., and Monroe, Elizabeth. *A History of Ethiopia.* Oxford: Clarendon Press, 1966.

Kalewold, Alaka Imbakom. *Traditional Ethiopian Church Education.* New York: Teachers College Press, 1970.

Kaplan, Irving et al. *Area Handbook for Ethiopia.* Washington, D.C.: United States Government Printing Office, 1971.

Kirkpatrick, Ivone. *Mussolini, A Study in Power.* New York: Hawthorne, 1964.

Laing, R. D. *The Politics of Experience.* New York: Ballantine, 1970.

Laitin, David D. "The Political Economy of Military Rule in Somalia." *The Journal of Modern African Studies* 14, no. 3 (1976): 449–468.

LaMotte, Ellen N. "A Coronation in Abyssinia." *Harper's Monthly Magazine* 162 (April 1931): 574–584.

Legesse, Asmarom. *Gada.* New York: The Free Press, 1973.

Legum, Colin. *Ethiopia: The Fall of Haile Selassie's Empire.* New York: Africana, 1975.

———. *Pan-Africanism.* New York: Frederick A. Praeger, 1965.

Leslau, Wolf. *Falasha Anthology.* New York: Schocken, 1969.

Levine, Donald N. *Greater Ethiopia.* Chicago: The University of Chicago Press, 1974.

———. *Wax and Gold.* Chicago: The University of Chicago Press, 1966.

Lewis, Herbert S. *A Galla Monarchy.* Madison: The University of Wisconsin Press, 1965.

Lewis, William H. "How a Defense Planner Looks at Africa." In *Africa: From Mystery to Maze*, edited by Helen Kitchen, pp. 277–309. Lexington, Mass.: Lexington Books, 1976.

Liebenow, J. Gus. "Which Road to Pan-African Unity?" In *Politics in Africa*, edited by Gwendolen M. Carter, pp. 1–32. New York: Harcourt, Brace and World, 1966.

Marcus, H. G. *The Life and Times of Menelik II.* Oxford: Clarendon Press, 1974.

Markakis, John. *Ethiopia, Anatomy of a Traditional Polity.* Oxford: Clarendon Press, 1974.

———. "Social Formation and Political Adaption in Ethiopia." *The Journal of Modern African Studies* 11, no. 3 (1973): 361–381.

Markakis, John, and Beyene, Asmelash. "Representative Institutions in Ethiopia." *The Journal of Modern African Studies* 5, no. 2 (1967): 193–219.

Mathew, David. *Ethiopia, The Study of a Polity 1540–1935*. London: Eyre and Spottiswoode, 1947.

Mosley, Leonard. *Haile Selassie: The Conquering Lion*. Englewood Cliffs, N.J.: Prentice-Hall, 1965.

Neumann, Sigmund. *The Future in Perspective*. New York: G. P. Putnam's, 1946.

Nkrumah, Kwame. *Handbook of Revolutionary Warfare*. New York: International Publishers, 1969.

Nyerere, Julius K. *Freedom and Unity*. London: Oxford University Press, 1967.

An Observer. "Revolution in Ethiopia." *Monthly Review* 29 (July–August 1977): 46–60.

Ottaway, David, and Ottaway, Marina. *Ethiopia, Empire in Revolution*. New York: Africana, 1978.

Ottaway, Marina. "Social Classes and Corporate Interests in the Ethiopian Revolution." *The Journal of Modern African Studies* 14, no. 3 (1976): 469–486.

Pankhurst, Richard. "Tribute, Taxation and Government Revenues in Nineteenth and Early Twentieth Century Ethiopia." *Journal of Ethiopian Studies* 5, no. 2 (July 1967): 37–87.

———. *An Introduction to the Economic History of Ethiopia from Early Times to 1800*. London: Lalibela House, 1961.

Paul, James C. N., and Clapham, Christopher, editors. *Ethiopian Constitutional Development*. Addis Ababa: Oxford University Press, 1967.

Perham, Margery. *The Government of Ethiopia*. Evanston, Ill.: Northwestern University Press, 1948; revised edition, 1969.

Phillips, Gene D. *Evelyn Waugh's Officers, Gentlemen, and Rogues*. Chicago: Nelson-Hall, 1975.

Redden, Kenneth R. *The Legal System of Ethiopia*. Charlottesville, Va.: Michie, 1968.

Schaefer, Ludwig F., editor. *The Ethiopian Crisis: Touchstone of Appeasement*. Lexington, Mass: D. C. Heath, 1961.

Scholler, Heinrich, and Brietzke, Paul. *Ethiopia: Revolution, Law and Politics*. Munich: Weltforum Verlag, 1976.

Schwab, Peter. "Cold War on the Horn of Africa." *African Affairs* 77, no. 306 (January 1978): 6–20.

———. *Decision Making in Ethiopia*. London: Christopher Hurst, 1972.

———. "Haile Selassie: Leadership in Ethiopia." *Plural Societies* 6, no. 2 (1975): 19–30.

———. "Human Rights in Ethiopia." *The Journal of Modern African Studies* 14, no. 1 (1976): 155–160.

———. "Rebellion in Gojam Province, Ethiopia." *Canadian Journal of African Studies* 4, no. 2 (Spring 1970): 249–256.

———. "The Tax System of Ethiopia." *The American Journal of Economics and Sociology* 29, no. 1 (January 1970): 77–88.

Schwab, Peter, editor. *Ethiopia and Haile Selassie*. New York: Facts on File, 1972.

Selected Speeches of His Imperial Majesty Haile Selassie I: 1918–1967. Addis Ababa: Ministry of Information, 1967.

Shack, William A. *The Gurage*. New York: Oxford University Press, 1966.

Shepherd, Jack. *The Politics of Starvation*. New York: Carnegie Endowment for International Peace, 1975.

Shneidman, J. Lee; Koz, Gabriel; and Levine-Shneidman, Conalee. "Catherine de Medicis." *Psychobiography* 1, no. 1 (February 1978): 3–15.

Silone, Ignazio. *Bread and Wine*. New York: Signet, 1963.

Skinner, Elizabeth, and Skinner, James. *Haile Selassie*. London: Thomas Nelson and Sons, 1967.

Smith, Denis Mack. *Mussolini's Roman Empire*. New York: Viking, 1976.

Stauder, Jack. *The Manjangir*. Cambridge: Cambridge University Press, 1971.

Stigand, C. H. *To Abyssinia Through an Unknown Land*. Philadelphia: J. B. Lippincott, 1910.

Surkin, Marvin, and Wolfe, Alan. *An End to Political Science*. New York: Basic Books, 1970.

Toynbee, Arnold. "A Tale of Sin and Nemesis." In *The Ethiopian Crisis: Touchstone of Appeasement?*, edited by Ludwig F. Schaefer, pp. 17–21. Lexington, Mass.: D. C. Heath, 1961.

Turner, Stansfield. "The Naval Balance: Not Just a Numbers Game." *Foreign Affairs* 55, no. 2 (January 1977): 339–354.

Uweche, Raph. "Our Fight Is With Those Opposed To The Masses." *Africa* (March 1978): 12–16. Interview with Lt. Col. Mengistu Haile Mariam.

Waugh, Evelyn. *When the Going Was Good*. New York: Penguin, 1951.

Wingerter, Rex. "The United States, the Soviet Union and the Indian Ocean: The Competition for the Third World." *Bulletin of Concerned Asian Scholars* 9, no. 3 (1977): 52–64.

Government Documents

The African Charter of Casablanca. United Nations, 1961.

Agriculture in Ethiopia. Compiled by H. P. Huffnagel. Rome: United Nations Food and Agriculture Organization, 1961.

Charter of the Monrovia Conference. United Nations, 1961.

Documents on International Affairs. Volume II. London: Oxford University Press, Humphrey Milford, 1937.

Ethiopia—Statistical Abstract. Addis Ababa: Central Statistical Office, 1965; 1966; 1970.

A *History of Kagnew Station and American Forces in Eritrea*. Information Division IACS-I. Headquarters, United States Army Security Agency. Arlington, Virginia, 1973.

Land Tenure Surveys of the Provinces of Arussi, Gamu Gofa, Shoa, Sidamo, Wollega, Wello, Eritrea. Addis Ababa: Ministry of Land Reform and Administration, 1967–1970.

Mann, H. S., and Lawrance, J. C. D. *Land Taxation in Ethiopia—Summary*. Addis Ababa: Ministry of Finance, 1964.

Negarit Gazeta. Decree No. 1 of 1942.

———. Proclamation No. 8 of 1942.

———. Order No. 1 of 1943.

———. Proclamation No. 60 of 1944.

———. Proclamation No. 70 of 1944.

———. Proclamation No. 117 of 1951.

———. Legal Notice No. 154 of 1951.

———. Proclamation No. 255 of 1967.

The 1931 Constitution of Ethiopia. Addis Ababa: *Ethiopia Observer*, V., No. 4 (1962): 362–365.

The 1955 Constitution of Ethiopia. Addis Ababa: *Negarit Gazeta*, November 4, 1955.

Public Papers of the Presidents of the United States. John F. Kennedy (1963). Washington, D.C.: United States Government Printing Office, 1964.

U.S. Congress, House of Representatives. *Foreign Assistance Act of 1969: Hearings.* Washington, D.C.: United States Government Printing Office, 1969.

U.S. Congress, Senate. Armed Services Committee. *Statement of James R. Schlesinger, Secretary of Defense,* June 10, 1975.

U.S. Congress, Senate. Committee on Foreign Relations. *U.S. Security Agreements and Commitments Abroad, Ethiopia.* Part 8, June 1, 1970.

Newspapers

The Ethiopian Herald.

The London Times.

The New York Times.

Vicker, Ray. "North Yemen Becomes One of Pivotal Nations In An East-West Tilt." *The Wall Street Journal,* June 2, 1977, 1, 22.

Index